Praise for *Worth It*

"Amanda Steinberg has done more toward educating women financially than anyone I know. She eloquently captures the pain and obstacles women face with money. Her stories are riveting. Her writing is inspiring. Her advice is brilliantly clear. I can't imagine anyone reading this without being deeply touched and highly motivated."

—Barbara Stanny, bestselling author of
Prince Charming Isn't Coming: How Women Get Smart About Money

"Amanda Steinberg gives us unvarnished assessments of sexism, our complex relationships with money, and her own path to taking control of her money and her life. Now, with Amanda's help, you will find the courage and the tools to make your money work for you."

—Becky Saeger, former financial services executive

"It's quite rare to find a book that so astutely meshes the emotional and practical aspects of mastering the money game. *Worth It* does this brilliantly. The insights within these pages are just what we need as women to wake us up from our money fog and get us firing on all cylinders. Read and apply this book— you and your life are worth it!"

—Kate Northrup, bestselling author of *Money: A Love Story*

"The reasons people mishandle money are far more deeply rooted than an absence of information, and many self-help books make things worse with intimidating how-to lists that don't address the real source of the problem. Salvation has finally arrived thanks to Amanda Steinberg, the founder of DailyWorth, who bridges the gap between technical know-how and emotional resistance with her brilliant new book, *Worth It*. Combining savvy nuts-and-bolts instruction with psychological insight smart enough to help even the most recalcitrant, *Worth It* is written in a warm, user-friendly tone that feels like your best girlfriend reassuring you instead of a scary math teacher yelling at you to do your homework. Money is power, and nobody can achieve real freedom without financial autonomy. *Worth It* shows the way for anyone to achieve the ultimate goal: Free At Last."

—Leslie Bennetts, author of *The Feminine Mistake* and
Last Girl Before Freeway: The Life, Loves, Losses,
and Liberation of Joan Rivers

"Amanda Steinberg is a champion for women and their relationship to money. She believes that in order to raise our net worth we must raise our self-worth. In her book *Worth It*, she guides us to step outside our comfort zone in order to step into financial freedom. This is a must-read if you want to live with confidence, abundance, and freedom."

—Gabrielle Bernstein, #1 *New York Times*
bestselling author of *The Universe Has Your Back*

"After a while, personal finance books all look the same. *Worth It* is not even in the same milieu. It changed how I think about my money, my future, and my life."

—Emma Johnson, personal finance journalist and founder,
WealthySingleMommy.com

"For all the finance books I've read, I've never felt so gotten as to my inner world around money and relationships. It's like dawn coming into deep unconscious, ancient patterns in my mind. And I know I'm not alone in this tangled darkness. This is going to be a landmark book—one that catalyzes liberation for women in their fullest expression of power and worth. This is how we rise."

—KC Baker, women's thought leadership coach and speechwriter, founder of WomanSpeak

NORTH
STAR
WAY

WORTH IT

WORTH IT

Your Life, Your Money,
Your Terms

AMANDA STEINBERG

NORTH STAR WAY
New York   London   Toronto   Sydney   New Delhi

NORTH STAR WAY An Imprint of Simon & Schuster, Inc.
1230 Avenue of the Americas
New York, NY 10020

First North Star Way hardcover edition February 2017

NORTH STAR WAY and colophon are trademarks of Simon & Schuster, Inc.

For information about special discounts for bulk purchases, please contact Simon & Schuster Special Sales at 1-866-506-1949 or business@simonandschuster.com.

The North Star Way Speakers Bureau can bring authors to your live event. For more information or to book an event, contact the North Star Way Speakers Bureau at 1-212-698-8888 or visit our website at www.thenorthstarway.com.

Interior design by Jaime Putorti

Manufactured in the United States of America

10 9 8 7 6 5 4 3 2 1

Library of Congress Cataloging-in-Publication Data is available.

ISBN 978-1-5011-4099-0
ISBN 978-1-5011-4101-0 (ebook)

To my mother and stepdad for always wrapping me
in unconditional love.

To my dad and stepmom, who gifted me the ultimate education
and strength to persevere.

To my sisters, who are also my best friends.

To Jordan, who made all of my wildest dreams our reality.

To Dylan and Maya, my mystical, magical angels.

To the women of DailyWorth, for believing in me and
our collective vision.

Contents

What Is a Woman's Worth?

Women are more powerful than ever in US history.
So what's wrong with our value?

Worthless. That's how I felt in my late twenties. I had bottomed out financially, emotionally—everything. I'd worked myself to the bone to showcase myself as a twenty-first-century working mom, and like practically every college-educated woman I knew, I had followed what seemed like straightforward steps to building the perfect postfeminist life. First, graduate from a good college. Second, find your passion. Third, land an impressive job in the field of your chosen passion. Fourth, find a supportive spouse or partner. Fifth, invest in real estate. Sixth, have a baby. Seventh, co-sleep, breast-feed, sleep-train the baby. Eighth, post a mix of happy, hilarious, and poignant pictures on Facebook and Instagram. Ninth, transition to your old job with reduced hours or your new full-time job allowing you to work at home (so you can be a stay-at-home-full-time-working mom). Tenth, keep earning the heaps of money commensurate with ambition and education to support your household. Eleventh, become a fulfilled mom and spouse, patron of good causes, and girls' soccer coach. Twelfth, sit throne-like on your laurels and relish self-satisfied bites of the fruits that your successful life program has produced. Cue the selfie!

I'd done everything right. Graduated from a top college? Check! Learned the lucrative skill of computer programming? Yes, ma'am! Worked eighty-hour weeks running a series of start-ups? Sure did, sisters! I married the sweetest man and became the mother of two very loved, very young children. Plus, I was a good earner. *Really* good: I made well beyond six figures. I'd done it. I'd pulled it off. From here on out, I figured, it was just a matter of coasting onto the smooth tarmac of security before officially arriving at the good life. All I had to do was to keep on making enough money to cover it. I would host fabulous dinner parties and creative playdates. My children, husband, and I would take culturally enriching vacations. My parents, siblings, extended family, colleagues, and friends would applaud the stunning perfection of my upper-middle-class feminist life. I wanted that life and I wanted that applause. So I continued to earn a lot of money. And I spent that money on nice cars (with hefty leases), a huge house (with huge utility bills), a nanny (I needed help while I was working), and nice work clothes (to be taken seriously in business). So as far as I was concerned, if I earned enough, spending was okay, and besides, my identity and sense of worth were attached to both. I was a big earner and a big spender: it's just who I *was*. Like the fabulous Carrie Bradshaw, I'd grown up with—and internalized—L'Oréal's repeat-after-me message to liberated American women: *I don't mind spending more . . . because I'm worth it.*

There were just a few problems with that logic. The emotional stamina and earning power required to sustain career and family was killer. Not only that, I couldn't afford our lifestyle, worth it or not. I owed walloping tax bills from the start-up businesses I'd run. My marriage was careening over the edge. Debt led to doubt; doubt spiraled into despair. I couldn't pull any of this off. I'd fallen for an advertising trick that masked reckless spending with women's empowerment. I'd been dead wrong about being "worth it." When it came down to it, I didn't really understand what worth meant at all.

But then, something saved me. As a former tweenage video game addict, I'd had my share of getting pummeled by bombs and monsters, hitting the reset button, starting over—and going on to win because I'd sharpened my strategy with every "death." And during my dark night of the soul, my inner tweenager saved me, whispering: *Hit the reset button, Amanda. Regenerate. Figure out your mistakes and capitalize on them. Look at the game in a whole different way by flouting conventional thinking. Start again. The game is never really over.*

So I did, slowly. I built myself back up, emotionally and financially. I created a new, more solid understanding of worth for my children and myself. I realized that *I* was in control of how this story turned out. So I changed it—to be specific, I changed my "money story." My money story, as it turned out, wasn't much different from my life story, from adolescence until getting snarled up in this plot twist as a "responsible adult." I realized that the story I'd been telling myself about my capacity to fund—to live—a good life was a fairy tale with a fated conclusion. In fact, *nothing* was predestined about my life. *No* magic moment of spousal support or family windfall was going to roust me from my depressive money coma and change my fortunes.

Wake up, sleeping beauty. I slapped myself. *Snap back to reality. You're in charge of creating whatever* happily ever after *means to you. You are the narrator of your own story.*

And so are you. You really are, and you really *can* do it, using something far more powerful than fairy dust or a magic kiss. Deploy your mind, your imagination—that part of you that longs to be *you.* But before we look at you in close focus, let's look at why it has been so difficult—so practically impossible—for women to take their own lives into their own hands, especially their money. We have—and we haven't—come a long way, baby.

Can't Be Ignored

Let's start with a basic question. What *does* worth mean for women? If you look at the economic reports of the past few years, we're worth more than ever in history. Women pretty much define the US economy now. That's not so newsy anymore. Women now hold the majority (52 percent) of management, professional, and related jobs in the US. Moreover, we're the primary breadwinners in more than 40 percent of American households—an almost fourfold increase since 1960. And when it comes to the US consumer economy, we make by far the majority of household spending decisions: 94 percent of home furnishings; 92 percent of US vacations; 91 percent of homes; 60 percent of cars; 51 percent of consumer electronics; and on it goes.[1] But women wield larger-scale economic power, too. We own 30 percent of all private businesses, employing more than nearly eight million Americans.[2] Globally, women hold an estimated 30 percent of private wealth. To a great degree, that wealth—which is expected to grow by 7 percent annually (that's *above* the global average)—is *self-made*.[3] The real kicker? Women currently control 51 percent, or $14 trillion, of personal wealth in the US and are expected to control $22 trillion by 2020.

Think of how much influence that is. That means we can decide not only which organic gluten-free soy chips to buy for little Aidan's and Ella's school lunches—or whether we'll vacation at Nana's this summer or practice Spanish as eco-tourists in Costa Rica—but also which companies, philanthropic organizations, political candidates, and humanitarian missions get our backing. We'll be able to vote with our dollars and investments. It means we can't be ignored. It means we can put our values front and center. Because if there's one thing we know for sure, it's that whoever holds the purse strings has the power. That's who says, "Yes, let's solve the malaria epidemic!" or "No, I won't support drilling for fossil fuels in what's left of our pristine wilderness." Or "Let's have universal health care, accessible day care, and better access to education, and provide help for parents at all stages." And so on—fill in your own blanks.

It's mind-blowing. Women have opportunities that never existed before at any point in history. We can choose when and with whom we want to have children—if at all. We can have sex lives unattached to marriage. We can choose our professions, our spouses, our homes, our property, and what we do with our money. But there's a fly in the soup. It's big, it's ugly, and we're still politely ignoring it.

Nowhere Near Enough

Women still lag behind men in the amount of earning power, savings, and wealth. It's true. Here we are, in the second decade of the twenty-first century. Women have more control over money than ever before. And we still have *nowhere near enough*.

As I write this, I'm looking at the latest US Bureau of Labor Statistics (BLS) numbers: Women now only earn 83 percent of what their male peers get paid.[4] The gap widens as women get older. Younger women (twenty to twenty-four years old) are closest to pay equity, earning 92 percent of what men do. In fact, until age thirty-five, women are paid about 90 percent of what men earn, according to a 2016 Catalyst survey.[5] But after that, median earnings for women start to slow down. Way down. The average full-time working woman will lose more than $460,000 over a forty-year period *due only to the pay gap*. Think about this. To catch up, she'll need to work an *extra twelve years*.

Women are also losing out on opportunities to invest in their futures. Big-time. Of the sixty-three million women (age twenty-one to sixty-four) working in the United States, just 44 percent invest in their employers' retirement plan, reports the US Department of Labor.[6] And after tallying up assets and subtracting debts, the simple but important formula describing a household's net worth, the US Census reports that female heads of household have a net worth of around $22,000; married couples have a net worth of about $140,000.[7] How can our potential for power be so great, even as our personal finances remain so comparatively low?

The Same Data

Since founding DailyWorth in 2009, I have come to see that the gender divide in long-term security is even greater than I had realized. While today's opportunities to manage and grow money are the same for both genders, the cultural mind-set is not. If you look at the research conducted by financial services companies, consulting firms, government agencies, and nonprofits on women and worth, you'll see that they all basically find the same data: men typically feel twice as confident as women making investing and financial decisions and say that they're primarily in charge of them, while women say that between work and family, they've got enough on their hands managing home economics.

How can we still have these sexist attitudes? Why haven't such tired old vestiges of the long-gone *Mad Men* era in American history shriveled up and died yet? Whenever I feel like my head is about to pop off with frustration from this, I have to remind myself: it's not that long gone. After all, the women's liberation movement only got traction after many of us were born. Think about this. The first Gen Xers (1965–1980) were newly minted babies when birth control for married couples became *legal in the United States*. A wife's job was to get pregnant. Until 1974, an American woman could not get a credit card from many banks without a male cosigner. It didn't matter if she was single or married. In the early 1970s, when the mayor of Davenport, Iowa—a woman—applied for a Bank of America credit card, she was denied. Unless her husband signed for it. Even up until *1981*, a man could legally get a second mortgage on a house he owned with his wife—without consulting her at all.

What seems outlandish now was status quo in the US, even within our own lifetimes. Moreover, all such sexist laws and social mores are more or less based on the *age-old* stereotype that women are somehow "hardwired" to emote and nurture, while men are "built" to reason and provide. And women have heard variations on *that* theme since . . . forever. *You don't need to—and, honestly, aren't able to—appreciate: the complexities of politics and voting; a college education, much less earning an advanced degree; what is required to work at high levels of business, academia, science, law, medicine, politics, and more; your role in human sexuality and reproduction, much less manage it.* And on it goes. We've been in a process of dismantling, and fighting against, the hydra of sexism for generations in this country. But the money piece somehow has been slow to shift. *Why* is the financial world so slow to catch up to reality? What's holding us up?

The Eight-hundred-pound Red Herring

For more than a decade, we've been told we are at fault. The earning and achievement gap persists, as the story goes, because educated, ambitious women "opt out" of their careers to take care of their families. Because we—and the whole world—know how impossibly perfectionistic contemporary American motherhood has become, it's tempting to believe that argument. But is it true? It is true that nearly 70 percent of primary caregivers in the US are women, whether bus drivers or CEOs. But of those, only 16 percent have been compelled to take on less-demanding jobs in order to also provide caregiving duties (compared with only 6 percent of male caregivers).[8] As for high-achieving women, the alleged mass exodus from office to home is starting to feel like the eight-hundred-pound red herring in the room.

A 2014 Harvard Business School (HBS) study, conducted by twenty-year veterans of research on professional women, found that out of more than twenty-five thousand HBS graduates surveyed, *only 11 percent were out of the workforce to care for children full-time.* The figure was less than half that for black women and women of South Asian descent (just 4 percent). Far from "opting out," the majority of Harvard MBA moms with children under eighteen living at home work full-time—to the tune of 74 percent of Gen X and 52 percent of Baby Boomer women. Indeed, research suggests that when high-achieving women leave their jobs after having children, only a tiny fraction want to be stay-at-home moms. The great majority of women quit as the final recourse to subtle sexist patterns in the workplace that had permanently "mommy-tracked" them. They'd been written off for using company flex time, taken out of the running for high-profile work, taken off projects they used to lead.

Further research has shown that women are systematically less likely to receive the kind of feedback in work reviews that they need to advance. A 2016 Stanford study found that because reviewers do not tie women's performance to specific business outcomes the way they do with men's, men get a clearer picture of what their perceived strengths are—and more guidance of exactly what they need to do to get to the next level.[9] Women are told when they are generally doing a good job, but reviewers tend to avoid naming incidences of when their work impacted business positively and what, particularly, the company values about their contributions. Vague feedback is correlated with lower performance review ratings for women—but not for men. In other words, vague feedback can specifically hold *women* back.

What's more, being stigmatized with the trait "bossy" is twice as likely to happen to women as it is men, a reputation that can have serious consequences for their careers, found a 2015 report published by the Center for Creative Leadership. Yet when managers were asked to describe a specific incident when they worked with someone "bossy," they were almost as likely to attribute bossiness to a man (48 percent) as they were a woman (52 percent).

Bossy women coworkers are rated as less popular than their bossy male peers—and rated less likely to have successful careers in the future. The study characterized the larger problem this way:

> When people think of leaders, they tend to think of men and stereotypically masculine traits (e.g., independence, aggression, competitiveness). Yet women are generally still expected to conform to stereotypically feminine traits (e.g., nurturing, nice, altruistic) in the workplace. This leads to a "double-bind" in which women who exhibit feminine traits are seen as lacking strong leadership qualities, while women who exhibit masculine traits are seen as unfeminine, mean, and unlikable.[10]

That kind of ham-fisted sexism plays out in no uncertain terms when women negotiate for a promotion with male bosses. A 2006 study jointly published by Harvard and Carnegie Mellon showed that evaluators penalize women far more than men for initiating salary negotiations, even for accepting company offers of higher compensation.[11] Male reviewers' "perceptions of niceness and demandingness explained resistance to female negotiators." Wait, *what*? Yep, they're saying that. "Look, women, don't you dare 'demand' a raise—or even accept one—from the Man because he doesn't think it's nice. And the Man doesn't like it when ladies don't act *nice* like they're *supposed* to." Wow. I had to read that a few times before I grasped how blunt discrimination often is. Yet there it is. Sexism in the workplace is literally preventing women from earning as much as their male counterparts—it happens all the time. What can women do to close the worth gap?

"Unbridled, Ruthless, Pathological"

We aren't exactly encouraged to engage. Bias is in the workplace—and all around us. Just think of the stereotypes about women and money. There's the princess who needs to be rescued. There's the frivolous spender. There's the gold-digging woman who's looking for a rich husband. The one I encounter a lot is the woman who just wants to be taken care of, pulled out of the workplace, and put on an allowance. We see gender differences in media portrayals, too. A TV ad called "Role Reversal" has a millennial-age son correcting his father about the way the investing world works today. In another ad, called "First Job," a young woman gets advice—from her father and his financial advisor—about setting long-term financial goals. The message is that women aren't good with money and aren't really interested it, not like men are. Money doesn't concern women and women shouldn't be concerned with money.

But the reality is different. Almost half of all MBAs today are awarded to women. We're not opting out. In spite of the facts, however, there's obviously a lingering bias against self-sufficient women. To be confident with money as a woman is to seem "demanding," not "nice." Money means power. Knowing how money works means power. But powerful women can be denied plum assignments and even raises; they're often seen as "bossy" and bad leaders. That's true even as women press for equal pay, a place at every decision-making table, and more top positions of government and management.

Just compare Hillary Clinton's 2016 bid for the Democratic nomination to her (male) competition. As Deborah Tannen, linguistics professor at Georgetown University, put it in her *Washington Post* analysis, when you search "ambitious + Bernie Sanders," you get headlines about "ambitious plans"; for Donald Trump, it's "ambitious deportation plan." But for Hillary, Tannen finds, Googling "ambitious" brings up very negative associations, such as "unbridled," "ruthless," and "pathological" ambition.

This idea echoes all around us, even in our most personal relationships. The 2015 Shriver report found that while heterosexual men are raising their daughters to be intelligent, independent, and strong, they married their wives because they were intelligent, attractive, and sweet. How do their daughters make sense of being taught to strive as they watch their mothers pressured to conform? Often, we strive to find a middle ground. We go for a job that's fulfilling enough, but we don't push for more responsibility or income—or it's denied us. We don't even really plump up our savings and investments so that we can have exactly what we want today and tomorrow.

Yes, making women's pay equal to men's will help solve some of these problems. So will providing better support for caregivers and taking more conscious steps to mentor young women. But ultimately these problems will truly be solved when more women are no longer afraid to manage their money. Money gives you choices. More income helps point you in the direction of safety and security. But true prosperity requires that women step into the role of the money manager without apprehension, guilt, fear, or shame. It's time. Owning your power and money means owning your worth.

Survey Says?

One important step is to take an inventory of our own biases. Some are easier to dismantle than you might think. For example, when all my flimsy, opposing values and beliefs about what was "worth it" finally came tumbling down in my late twenties, one of the first, easiest decisions that I made was to brainwash myself—productively, rather than destructively. Since I had set a major bias against myself by telling myself I was a *spender*, I started to tell myself that I was a *saver*. I was broke, believe me, but every time I had change in my bag or pocket, I'd drop it into a jar in my kitchen and telepath myself a cheerful Jedi mind trick: *I just saved. See? I am a saver!* I'm not going to tell you that doing this permanently saved the day; I'll still slide in and out of debt when life goes haywire. But because I practiced that simple act of saving and note-to-self regularly over time, my default MO is now to save before I spend.

"I Was Raised Not to Talk About Finances"

Some biases are intrinsic to our outlook because they are tightly knit into our culture. We might never be able to erase these completely, but we can be aware of them and check our reactions so that we don't allow them to interfere with productive thinking and behavior.

Consider the results of a 2016 Fidelity study. Most of the women surveyed (82 percent) were confident managing household finances and budgeting. But their self-assurance plummeted when asked if they could handle planning for their long-term financial needs (37 percent) or selecting the right financial investments (28 percent). Their psychological contortions are almost painful to read. Even though almost all wanted to know more about financial planning (92 percent), and three-quarters wanted to learn more about money and investing, most women said that they'd refrained from discussing their finances with the people closest to them, including family and friends (80 percent). Reasons? Roughly a third agreed with these statements: *It's uncomfortable* or *I was raised not to talk about finances.*

In most of the discussions today about women's advancement, money is still missing, caught between gender lines. Yet attempts to rebalance the discussion today—to propose that women can manage money *and enjoy it*—still tend to threaten even our unconscious beliefs about how marriage and family should operate. Let's face it: a good, feminine, desirable woman of worth cannot honestly discuss money or business without threatening her relationships. As Millionaire Matchmaker Patti Stanger said in a 2015 interview: "I like to tell women to be alpha at work and beta at home. It takes practice. If you're used to running your life and you scared all the men away, you might have to go beta Suzy Homemaker at home and really go hot to switch gears and detox, because most alpha men do not like an alpha woman telling them what to do."

Never Second-Guessed It

But that approach can backfire, too. Let me tell you a story.

My friend Steph Wagner had a fairy-tale romance with her college sweetheart, whom she later married. She graduated at the top of her class in finance with the goal of being a Wall Street analyst. In her twenties and into her thirties, she really did seem to have it all: a balanced and happy marriage; a big job (at twenty-five, she was working in private equity as a vice president); the respect of her peers; and soon, a growing family that was very well off. After her first child, her boss let her work part-time, but then she was expecting her second child. "They asked me to get on a Cessna when I was six months pregnant and had a two-year-old at home," Steph told me. "That was it. I decided to quit."

She and her husband made what she calls a business decision. "We thought about what was best for our family, what was best for his career. It was well thought out, and I never second-guessed it, never thought, *Oh shit—what am I doing?* I never had one ounce of distrust in my husband—never thought I was at risk." In fact, she lived the busy life of an extremely bright and motivated stay-at-home mom of three boys in a wealthy family. "I ran the home so he could travel two hundred nights a year and not worry about anything." Until eighteen years into their marriage, when the "business" decision fell apart.

One night Steph learned that her husband was living a double life: he'd been having an affair for almost three years. She spent an agonizing year and a half trying to save the relationship, the family, the life they'd had. But it didn't work. He moved out of the house and out of the state, leaving Steph to sort through the emotional and financial wreckage of her life—and take complete responsibility for the children, not having worked for fourteen years. She had it all and had done it all "right." Her life had seemed handled. Until it just wasn't. And she wasn't ready for it.

Hey, if your financial strategy is to marry rich—I wish you the best possible outcome. Just please promise me this—if you marry someone of means, you need to run the household books alongside them. You need to be clear on what you own as a marital unit and where the money is going. When you understand your financial worth—when you declare it and redeclare it— you'll *want* to be involved. The more you engage, the more you understand, the more you can codirect how your life goes. For women, it's the new normal.

Depending on where you live, what you and your spouse acquire during marriage (including assets) becomes marital property in the case of divorce. However, the rules vary state to state, and it's complicated to tease out the real value of property and assets, especially if the divorce is contentious. You need to know what's going on. All too often, what happens is the partner takes over, and because you are not participating, you get blindsided when there's trouble. And, boy, can there be trouble.

Barbara Stanny, in her book *Overcoming Underearning*, tells the tragic story of ignoring her net worth. As the daughter of one of H&R Block's founders, Stanny had a sizable inheritance. When she married, she handed over the financial reins to her husband. She checked out, thinking he would take care of their wealth. Instead, the worst possible thing happened. Her husband not only gambled away most of her money—and he was a *financial advisor!*—but he also left her a million-dollar bill for unpaid taxes. Divorced, she was hugely in debt and had children to care for. She'd ignored money until she was in very big trouble.

Having It Handled

Divorce can be a major curveball, but others are possible, even likely. Like trusting your retirement's asset allocation to a financial advisor, only to lose more than half in a crash too close to your retirement. The truth is, expenses have this magical way of blossoming far beyond what you project. Stability ebbs and flows. Your kid suddenly needs a cell phone and data plan. Travel soccer costs two thousand dollars. It happens every month, every week—you dent your rental car (I did this TWICE this year); your dad can't afford his medication; your child needs a tutor. You need an operation: to remove that part of your ear that can hear kids and bosses whining. We digress . . . all of these are expensive and disruptive—and normal. To me, *having it all* means *having it handled*. Everything is covered, because you're set up like a boss to handle it. That's where we're going.

In my experience, *having it handled* also means reaching for an impossible goal—something that lights me up with the thrill of the unattainable. That is, it's something to really stretch for, the way that some of our grandparents (or even parents) put a ton of time into planning, saving, and strategizing to move to this country or buy their own homes. By dreaming big and setting absurd goals, my ambitions swell, and money becomes inspiring, not drudgery.

Life doesn't go in a straight line from leaving school, to making money, to having a family and retiring. And because of this—because of how we *thought* our lives would go and what we felt entitled to—we feel like we're doing things wrong, like we've made a mistake. Things are not working out, and *it's our fault.* But that's a trap. And it's totally demoralizing and unmotivating. You're riding a wave between storms, not climbing the stairway to heaven. Got it?

We Need Money

Traditional mores may help explain social attitudes that distance women from money, but there are a whole lot of practical reasons that do the job, too. A 2016 Prudential study found that women flat out don't have enough money to put toward long-term financial goals. In fact, almost a third of those surveyed cited a lack of disposable income as their biggest financial planning hurdle. Also, many women, to quote the study, "admit to a lack of familiarity with financial products and the industry jargon used to describe them, and a sense that they simply don't know what to consider when evaluating the financial options available to them." They just don't have the time to figure it out, they say.[12]

I'm telling you now: bullshit on all of this. If you ate today, you have money to save. If financial products confuse you, start with a separate savings account. Don't think you have time? Wake up one hour earlier. You have the funds, brains, and time to change your financial position—this book is going to make that crystal clear. You must make time to play with money options so that you have more, not less, when you need it. Some 90 percent of women in the US will at some point be entirely on their own financially. The idea that men are providers and women are taken care of isn't reality anymore. Only 23 million of 111 million US households look like the traditional nuclear family structure. The majority looks more like, well, me: single-parent household managing work, kids, and coparenting.

When it comes to basic life stuff—the ability to buy a home, own a car, care for children, save for retirement, move to a new home—more money means more choices. Having the power to choose can mean that you're not trapped in a bad public school system, stuck in a dead-end job, or trying to live off social security alone. When it comes to money, it's essential that women know how to make it, save it, plan with it, invest it, stretch it, grow it, enjoy it, and share it. But until now we either haven't wanted to disrupt our status as dependent members of our families, or we've felt overwhelmed by trying to understand how money works. Or we've so fully accepted the idea that our lives can only look like they do right now—or will be "fixed"—that we don't challenge our own status quo. We lack a sense of creativity over money—and how we think about money.

It's not that many women are not diligent savers, budgeters, and investors. According to a DailyWorth survey of four thousand women in August 2015, 50 percent of responders felt in control of their day-to-day finances. But that also means that 50 percent did not. It's not enough. We *all* need to feel—and to be—in control of our finances because money dictates our destinies. If you are cringing right now, let me repeat that there is no shame here. Yes, we have to dismantle what we've been taught and rebuild our lives, our philosophies, our authentic *selves*, with financial knowledge. But we have in no way lost. Far from it. We have enormously exciting opportunities right *now*.

So let the gatekeepers of the fading social orders say—like *Esquire* editor David Granger did in the "How to Be a Man" issue (June/July 2013)—that "the gender gap is widening to the detriment of men." We're already increasingly in the driver's seat. The transition is already under way. Your life, your freedom, your choices, and your security are on the line. The truth is, we don't even know the half of it. We don't even comprehend what is possible.

It's Worth It

Let's put blame and shame on the bonfire. Let's put aside the basics like budgeting, debt strategies, and 529s, and take a big step back. Many of us are still caught in some form of rescue fantasy where either extreme budgeting, getting married, or building a successful business will finally set you free. That was true for me. I didn't think my husband would save me, but I believed my earning power would. Wrong. But first I had to go through the fairy tale to come out the other side. So can you.

The reason I started DailyWorth, and the reason that I wrote this book, is because I've lived through the delirium of hamster-wheel career mom, all the while telling myself that I was living an ideal life. But I came to realize that even though it looked like I was running a million miles a second—and I was—I was actually under a busyness spell, optimistic that big, hairy problems would soon be solved, without any clear pathway to resolution. If this sounds even a little like you, I want to help.

Throughout this book, I am going to help you face your fears about managing money—and your life. Just as I did myself.

You've been telling yourself a story about yourself and money. I did, too. I want to help you dismantle it and figure out how and why you were shackled to a script that you followed line for line for four years or forty. Then we're going to shred it, we're going to burn it, and we're going to emerge from those ashes.

You're going to come out fresh and ready to learn what you need to know: to move from just earning enough to building solid assets that you can use to fund your life. We're going to make you strong, train you to operate in reality—*your* reality, as it is. We're going to dig deep. We're going to clean your haunted financial house from top to bottom. I'm going to hit the reset button along with you. You are going to regenerate as the woman you actually want to be, living the life you actually want to live, on your own terms.

I promise: it's worth it. Let's do it now.

PART 1

Your Life: Telling Stories

How your life story is also about you and your money.

CHAPTER 1

Hit the Reset Button.

The (money) story of my life: what I learned, when I rose, why I fell, and how I started all over again from scratch.

There's something extracruel about adolescence. It's arguably the most insane time of a girl's life. To begin with, you had to survive raging hormones, your mind-body transformation, *and* the relentless *coup d'états* within tweenage girls' social ranks. In the midst of this turmoil, it turns out that you also began forming your core identity—by telling yourself a story. It turns out that a primary way we make sense and meaning of our lives over time is by internally penning a "personal narrative," according to a growing body of psychological research. It's your life story according to you, though deciding on major themes or choosing which memories to keep or toss is not a conscious process. It's our budding psyches' way of describing who we are to ourselves and in the world, why and how we got that way, and what our futures can, or will, look like. As life goes on, you *become* the story you tell about yourself. And not surprisingly, a big piece of that story is about money.

Money started out as a game to me—a video game, to be

specific. Nintendo's Kid Icarus was my nemesis throughout my tweenhood, and to beat it required tactical maneuvers to increase one's chief assets, pixelated gold "coins." You played a character called Pit, a winged boy equipped with a bow and arrows. Your job was to free the goddess by collecting the three "sacred" treasures guarded by monsters. To defeat them, you, Pit, had to zap them with your powerful arrows. And to build up your store of powerful arrows, you needed to amass and manage an ample supply of gold coins. You also needed "hearts" to give you the strength to do what needed to be done. It sounds like the ultimate geek fairy tale now, but let me tell you: getting to the happy ending was *not* easy. At all. And it consumed me for the better part of my adolescence.

Month after month, the monsters outmaneuvered me, depleted my arsenal, and ripped at my wings. I, Pit, would invariably die. My winnings, my progress, my life: Boom! Gone, just like that. You'd think that I'd give up after taking sound beatings for a couple of weeks. It never occurred to me. On the contrary, I became a more confident and skillful Pit because I knew what all players know: the game is never really over. You can always hit the reset button. In fact, when you start over again, you improve your score each time—and not simply because you've learned from earlier mistakes and know best how to increase and manage your critical assets. The major reason you jump levels is almost always because you risked an untried strategy—and it worked. When it does, you suddenly see with new clarity and depth how the game is played. You can't *wait* to hit that reset button.

So, as I learned to shoot with increasing precision, I started to power-spike through the first spate of levels, facing bigger, meaner monsters. And finally, after two solid years of playing, I beat Kid Icarus. I won. I'd mastered this game. I knew how to regenerate from loss and start over. I knew how to learn from my mistakes and to strategically deploy my knowledge. To build up my assets. To gain dexterity and build confidence. Take calculated risks. Be ready to cope with the unexpected, no matter what. See how it all worked from a completely different—and optimal—vantage point.

It's both weird and inspiring to me, looking back on it now. I mean, on the one hand, here I was, a punk kid soaking up the glory of my newfound ass-kicking skills. But on the other, I came to value deeply those same ass-kicking skills as an adult. Ultimately, they became the fundamental principles undergirding my philosophy of managing money—and the same skills I would use years later, when I reinvented myself and began building solid financial worth for myself and my kids.

But I didn't see my gamer skill set as valuable, even lifesaving, in the real world for a long, long time—and after a great deal of pain and soul-searching. That quest was no Kid Icarus. It started in my own life. It started with my mom.

Support Yourself

When my parents divorced in the early 1980s, there was no such thing as "conscious uncoupling." Divorce was all but unheard-of in conservative suburban Philadelphia. There was no cultural acceptance of it, no narrative of psychological recovery from it. *Divorced* was not in my mom's cultural lexicon until my father moved out. My mother was raised to be the worthy woman of the 1950s: the diligent housewife and center of the organized, loving home. She was a good girl from a good family. For her, a successful life story was straightforward: you married well; raised attractive, competent children; and supported your husband's needs and career. In return, you were rewarded with a secure, comfortable life and a sense of personal fulfillment. Even privileged women who had been sent to college, like my mother, typically acknowledged that their chief goal was to graduate with an "MRS. degree." When my father divorced her, Mom lost more than her husband. She lost her identity. She went from "priceless" to abandoned.

With three daughters and no job prospects, Mom was stunned. My two older sisters—one eleven years older, the other eight years—and I watched as the "good girl" melted down. The foundation Mom had built over years ruptured in a matter of months. I'd often find her crying on the edge of her bed in her dimly lit bedroom. One day, she snapped and gripped my scrawny biceps, telling me: "Always be able to support yourself financially."

Meanwhile, my dad, a successful surgeon, remarried and lived with my new stepmother and her children in a stunning house with a small fleet of cars. When I visited my dad on weekends and vacations, I could only see what I didn't have: a fancy home, a glittering pool, a family that I wished was mine. I marinated in jealousy, grief, and resentment. Cue the first themes in my personal narrative: Husbands and fathers won't save you; they might not even stick around. Be independent, earn a lot of money, and buy your own cars and house. The way to heal is living well.

Really Different

Meanwhile, Mom began to emerge. It took her years to lose that glazed-over postdivorce look, but when she did, she did it with stunning determination. Her undergraduate degree in the sixties had been in math and physics. She'd even done computer programming. "Computers filled entire rooms, and we used punch cards," she told me. Now she went back to graduate school, earning an MBA from Drexel in information systems (high-tech eighties speak). After graduating, she got a job putting together personal computers via mail order. She filled our garage with thick beige monitors and CPUs with floppy disk drives, computer parts awaiting assembly. Then she took on a bigger job, working at the Philadelphia Stock Exchange on its first computer help desk. She started a career at forty-two years old. Boom. Mom hit the reset button. *Game on.*

To avoid a two-hour commute, she moved us to downtown Philadelphia. We settled into a town house on a cobblestone street dating back to Philadelphia's colonial era. Our neighborhood, known as South Street, was also the punk mecca of bohemian Philadelphia in 1989. It was gritty. Our new neighbors were the back doors of restaurants. Steam from hot kitchens and waiters on smoke breaks. After ten years of reclusive life in the suburbs, this shift into urban adventure was exhilarating. My mother and her career took off. She'd pump up the volume—the Talking Heads song "Burning Down the House" was a favorite—and we'd dance on the dining room table. She was *laughing.*

If it was liberating for her, it was also liberating for me. Mom gave me a lot of freedom, much more than most kids my own

age. No curfew, no limits on TV or sugared cereals. When my
twelve-year-old self came home with new ear piercings and dyed
hair, Mom didn't worry. But I did. I began to realize how different Mom and I were from everyone else. My other friends
weren't allowed to do things like this. Their families had one
boy, one girl, married parents, a welcoming home. The mother
would be warm and intellectual, loving and strict. The father,
when he was at home, was genial but firm. They loved each
other. My friends had chores, books their parents had assigned
them to read, family dinners where they discussed those books.
Their parents hosted interesting dinner parties with interesting people; their families took culturally enriching vacations.
I wanted this family. I wanted this life. This was the idealized
family life: the peaceful, well-ordered home run by a worthy
woman and benevolent patriarch, populated by smart, engaged
kids. They lived by the rules.

Whatever Obstacles

Subconsciously, I was hoping that Mom would draw the line
and enforce "normal" family rules. She didn't have any use for
"normal" back then, though. "Normal" had left her stranded in
the suburbs, an outsider among married couples. She was re-
generating herself as a mother and woman, the quantum-leap
version of hitting the reset button. Her identity was no longer
wrapped up in a man's valuation of her as "priceless" or anything else. She was developing and evaluating her own worth.
And starting over made her promote her newfound philosophy.
"Roots and wings—roots to know you have a family who loves
you and a secure home, and wings to chart your own path, the

confidence to face whatever obstacles may get in your way," she'd tell me. "Yes, you'll fly right into storms and get thrown around a bit. But you'll be fine. I believe in you."

I was thrown around all right. I wandered and prowled at will. When our thirteen-year-old neighbor offered to pay me twenty-five dollars for a hand job, I accepted. More than once. Hey, having grown up in an all-female household, I was curious about boy parts. I also wanted to buy one of the expensive crystal necklaces that everyone had at school. It seemed like a fair trade at the time. I'd hop on the SEPTA (public) bus and ride deep into West Philly, where I learned to talk my way in and out of awkward teenage experiments. I acted and reacted on my feet: Pit on the street.

Enter a new theme in my personal narrative: *I need family, traditions, a sense of normalcy.* I wanted that well-ordered peaceful home with the thriving children and admiring husband, where my contributions would support our family and create a prosperous environment. Even as I knew, perhaps, it wasn't really my life. Even then, I knew I'd never grow up to become the archetypal "good wife." I would have to create a different kind of home, be a different kind of mother, wife, woman, so that I would feel comfortable, fulfilled—not an impostor in my own life. I knew that I would soar and crash again and again—but I would always pull myself back up, hit reset, and regenerate.

Real Money

My mother's warning to my five-year-old self was my North Star—and it would become the core of my identity. I didn't expect to be taken care of. I didn't yearn for a man—or a boss—

to provide for me. That felt like prison. So in my senior year of college in Manhattan, I was making forty dollars an hour programming databases for college administrators. That was crazy money for a college kid. I was one of the first to buy a cell phone and take a spontaneous vacation to St. Barths. The year I graduated, 1999, the Internet exploded, and I convinced the CEO of a Boston-based website programming company to let me open a New York City office under his established brand. He thought I was far too young, but I ignored him and did it anyway. I was going to make real money now.

But hold up a minute. As unconventional and tenacious as I was, I ached for love, children, and my own fairy-tale version of sustainable Zen living. So, in my early twenties, I strategically frequented bars, parties, and even Shabbat dinners (oy—I'm not even religious) until I met my match. The One was a psychotherapist, PhD, yogi, and a drummer: the perfect yin to my yang of money and tech. We united, threw a killer postmodern wedding bash, birthed a baby boy, and moved to Philly. Life finally felt normal. Now I had a marriage and a family. We also needed the right house to complete our episode of *The Wonder Years: The Dot-Com Years*. The house we bought was the starter version of an English manor. I was finally living well.

The problem was, I secretly had no idea how to manage any of it: Our income, lifestyle, and savings that created financial security. Investments that created worth and wealth. Granted, we were young, but I talked a big game—I *played* a big game. By age twenty-five, I hit six figures. But I didn't know a thing about money except how to work to earn it. I didn't know that I was actually digging myself into a big financial hole. By age thirty, I would end up almost $100,000 in debt.

Never Enough

For the time being, though, our home looked well ordered. You couldn't tell we had problems. But the costs were adding up fast. First, my computer programming business, Soapbxx (the domain name "Soapbox.com" was already registered), got a $60,000 bill for back taxes. That was triple the amount I had paid the previous year. The business was growing rapidly, and profits were increasing—but I hadn't adjusted my taxes. When you're self-employed, you have to file taxes quarterly. I'd been paying taxes for my previous year's earnings but been too delirious with work and young children to recognize that a jump in revenues would mean a jump in taxes, too. My business had cashflow issues. Our clients often paid late, and we owed vendors thousands of dollars. The company checking account had $2,000 in it. Not nearly enough to pay for anything.

Our stone manse wasn't helping, either. The cost of repairing and maintaining a big, 100-year-old house was steep. The heating bills alone were $1,000 a month. The crumbling windows cost $10,000 to replace. The mortgage payments on a $700,000 home were humungous. Raising a child was much more exhausting and expensive than I'd anticipated. There wasn't enough money to pay any of these bills. There was never enough.

Then I became pregnant with our second child, a baby girl. A boy and a girl! But . . . I wasn't prepared for the *even more intense* exhaustion and stress of having a newborn *and* a toddler. And the social pressure to be the perfect mother—to breast-feed, practice attachment parenting, avoid TV before age two—clashed with work pressure. During work, I'd get called by day care to pick up a sick child. On weekends, a client would call in a broken Web page. We had to spend, spend, spend to hire more help at work, more help at home, and try not to lose our minds in the process. Crushing, gutting, frantic. It dawned on me that I was Pit from Kid Icarus again, with no coins and no hearts left. Except I was all grown-up and couldn't hit a button to start over.

A Riff on Cinderella

Some knowledge of basic money management would have helped. How should I properly calculate the true cost of owning a home? How do I create savings when I have so much debt? It's not that I didn't *want* to save money. But the three-ring circus of earning money, baby-rearing, and keeping up with monstrous heating bills never seemed to leave me much to work with. *I'll just keep working harder*, I told myself, pouring another glass of wine.

We budgeted. I set up a Mint account. It took hours to re-program it to autocategorize each expense into a clearly delineated category. "Kids." "Gifts." But wait, what about gifts for kids? Where does that expense go? And we're out of money, but if we show up to Yael's birthday party without a gift, will we be bad community members and shunned from future birthdays? Only when I was done did I realize that there was no way that *budgeting* was going to get me out of that mess. I needed a framework: a new paradigm. As luck would have it, right as my personal financial crisis was hitting home, I got an e-mail about a workshop on women and money. "Is it possible to maintain integrity, build wealth, *and* make a difference?" the e-mail asked.

Please let the answer be yes, I thought. The workshop was to be led by old friends of mine: a hip-hop artist and entrepreneur named Rha Goddess, and a spiritually elevated human rights advocate, Lea Endres. We'd be "shattering the glass ceiling & other myths about why women won't claim money, power, and respect." I needed this.

So, on a hot September day, at six months pregnant, I took the train from Philadelphia to New York City, desperate for new insights on money. In the workshop, I realized how my own "money story"—my personal narrative and identity around money—was driving me. My money story had told me that financial freedom was the key to the good life, and that meant working hard and making a lot of money. But once I had the money, I had no idea what to do with it. I had no savings, no appreciating investments, nothing that made my actual financial *worth* more than that of my teenage self. My "assets" (i.e. real estate, business) were actually driving me into debt. My money story had told me that I was going to build a secure, prosperous home with my husband. But I had no emergency fund and no safety net to catch me if I ever fell off the high wire during my precarious balancing act. And I did fall.

What had gone wrong? I had been following the personal narrative I'd written in adolescence, but I hadn't edited it for adulthood. I hadn't listened when my inner wisdom was cuing me to shift focus, to reengineer the arc of my story to form a bridge to authentic freedom—not a slide to self-destruction.

My money story was actually a riff on *Cinderella*: weird, wild, isolated girl is magically saved by her own ambition, Prince Supportive, their children, and expensive stuff.

That fairy tale crashed and burned—with massive financial consequences. Even though I learned not to be dependent like my mother, I still ended up in horrible financial trouble like she did.

Leaving the workshop, I had another epiphany. Money doesn't have to be the source of so much anxiety or stress. It can also be a source of freedom, power, and choices in our lives. This can be true regardless of our financial circumstances—whether we have $100,000 in debt or $1,000,000 in the bank. It is not just about how much you have or don't have. It all depends on how you handle it. Curveballs in life (children, divorce, death, lay-offs, moving) are constant, but the way you position yourself to catch those curveballs can be strategic and consistent. You'll be fine. *If* you have a healthy money story and *if* you're not afraid to engage.

Terrible Clarity

Sometime after I gave birth to my daughter, Maya, I realized my marriage was in trouble. I had married the sweetest man, but slowly I'd been discovering that I didn't fit into the role of "wife." Or at least the wife we had both wanted. He'd married a woman he loved, only to find that my drive and ambition made me a pretty terrible companion. When I should have been snuggling up to watch a movie or helping to plant the vegetable garden, I was instead hiding in the bathroom to answer e-mails. Our financial stress pushed me into work. So I created further projects to contract. I was doing anything I could to try to pay our mounting pile of bills—a Sisyphean task.

Even after the workshop, I was still sure something was seriously wrong with me. I had tried different therapies to deflate my oversized ambition. My drive and aspirations were problems—clearly they were hurting my marriage. I wanted to love being an attentive mom, loving wife, and gracious hostess. I wanted to create that priceless home, in all senses. But I didn't. I hated what it took to be all those things at once. There were so many rules and social norms to adhere to, so many ideas of right and wrong. I didn't want to follow any of them. I'd been raised by a liberated single mother, given a long leash, and I went where I wanted to go. And with terrible clarity, it hit me: I didn't want to be *here*. I sobbed and sobbed with grief—and relief. I knew that I had to deconstruct and rebuild my life anew.

So I took a couple hundred deep breaths and moved out. I left our pristine home for a dingy two-bedroom apartment a few blocks away for my kids and me. It had a parquet floor, peeling linoleum paneling, and thin walls, but I could afford it. I bought a used 2004 Toyota hatchback. I started cutting and dyeing my own hair. I went DIY across the board. I felt embarrassed by such radical downsizing. But I could breathe again.

For the first time in my adult life, I had cash. I was finally going in the right direction, freeing myself from bills, meeting my expenses. I could see a day when I'd be building savings and investments. And I made DailyWorth my therapeutic creative outlet. I wanted women to get this new message about money: that it could be plentiful, nourishing, and within their (my) grasp.

Life on Your Terms

Today, I rent a small house with a fireplace and arched windows. I have made peace with not being "normal." I put my savings account ahead of social expectations, and my investment account ahead of more clothes. As Lea and Rha taught me, what you want doesn't start by creating a budget. It starts with your money story.

I've just told you mine. Now let's get to yours.

CHAPTER 2

Rewrite Your Story.

Wake up, Sister. Time to take this
story in a different direction.

In 2006, Nisha Moodley left her career in cosmetics. For nine years, she'd been rising steadily through the industry, taking on more responsibility. She enjoyed a good salary and benefits. But she wanted to serve women in a deeper way. So she jumped. She put herself through nutrition school and launched a coaching business to help women overcome emotional eating. In just a few years, she was earning far more than she ever had, and she was doing what she loved. Success! Or was it? In spite of her high earnings, she wasn't saving a dime. The more she earned, the more she spent. She lived well, but she had no safety net.

Elle Satto learned the hard way how much damage *what she didn't know* could do. As a young woman, she believed that checks were a "promise to pay" at some time in the future, not a withdrawal of cash right now. "Those checks I wrote all over town were so rubber. It was a mess. I was wildly overdrawn and I couldn't pay all those NSF fees," Elle told me. "That cemented my relationship with money." Elle dropped out of school and started working full-time to replenish her bank account. She didn't know what else to do. Growing up, her mother had handed off money to her father to manage. "That just continued a vicious cycle of not learning about money in my family," she said.

Rachel Bellow, cohost of the podcast *The Big Payoff*, catches herself believing she can spend her way into the life she wants. "I believe that *this* purchase will change my life. This pair of jeans, these shoes. I will see an amazing outfit—that I will not wear, because I do not have the life that goes with that outfit—and yet I hear myself say, 'You know? If I bought that dress, and I'm on a cruise ship in the Caribbean, with that guy who has that awesome beard . . . ' And all of a sudden I'm in this fantasy of the life that would justify that purchase."

Tara Gentile's money story had to do with earning money. Tara was thrifty and hardworking. No debt, no trouble with banks or overspending. But she was a classic underearner. She was satisfied if she had *just* enough money to get by. "My mom said, 'You can be anything you want, but that might not always make much money—and that's okay.'" So Tara worked in a big chain bookstore for $14 an hour. "Not only was I underpaid—I was smart! I'd been a PhD student!—I truly thought I'd never make more than $45,000 a year."

If any of these stories resonate with you, then you, too—like Nisha, Elle, Rachel, and Tara (and me)—have a money story that needs an edit. Because chances are, it's running your financial life.

My Prince Will Come

I told you my entire money story in the last chapter—and it wasn't all that different from my personal narrative: my life story. The only difference is that when I looked at my formative experiences and major turning points, I focused on what I was learning about money and how it affected my life and identity. The same is true for you. Your money story is all your unconscious beliefs you have about money—how you should earn it, what it means to want it, and what it means to have a lot or a little. It reveals a lot about yourself and what you believe is possible. In my workshops, I ask women to start by telling me their money story in one sentence. It's easier than being asked to write your entire autobiography, for one thing. But for another, condensing your story to a one-liner makes you think carefully about the major arc of your story—and what you believe about yourself and the way you engage with money. Here are some more common ones:

"Money lets me buy whatever I want."
"No matter how hard I try, I can't save."
"In a recession, asking for a raise can get you fired."
"Money is evil."
"Someday, my prince will come."

When Nisha heard about money stories in one of my workshops, she began to explore her own. Nisha's money story? She was not saving because she was waiting to be saved. By a man. Or a start-up. Someone or something that wasn't her. Uh-oh. "I was married to a musician," she reflected. "I hoped that he would win a record deal or something that would save us financially." Even though she earned great money, she dismissed the intention to hold on to it.

Our unhealthy money stories operate in the background of our minds and undermine our lives. Nisha believed that if she was too good with money—if she had "full sovereignty" over it, as she puts it—she'd have to give up her femininity. She'd have to be responsible for everything, and would never get the support she craved in life. She believed that she needed to stay uninformed and unconscious about money in order to be happy.

Something Deeper at Play

Many of us go through our adult lives not understanding our money. We don't see money as an interesting or valuable game to play. Instead we disassociate from our finances. Or we avoid them. In our guts, we know we can't really rationalize disengaging, but somehow we feel happier by not dealing. Here are some other one-liner money stories I hear from women:

> "I'm a creative, nonlinear thinker. I leave money to others."
> "My husband loves managing our investments. I can't do it all. I just don't have the brain for it."
> "Capitalism is evil. So I don't get caught up in it."

It's ironic that turning off the part of our brains that thinks about money makes us feel better. And that mishandling our money and putting ourselves in harm's way seems more satisfying than opening our statements, looking at our options, and really seeing where we are. The underlying truth is that just the thought of looking at what money and assets we *have* and what we *want* fills us with dread. But why?

Many women believe that they are inherently worse than men at math or quantitative thinking. We believe that managing money requires too many complex formulas. Or that a false move can become a costly mistake. Or threaten our key relationships or family roles. And there doesn't seem to be a compelling reason to engage. Won't someone eventually handle it for us? If we keep waiting for financial rescue, then we don't have to face any confirmation that we're incompetent at it. Or excellent at it. But the truth is that managing money is not highly technical. You do not need an advanced degree to engage. It's not that we *can't* understand what's before us. There's something deeper at play. It's our beliefs around money—everything it means to have money (or not have it) that we can't stomach.

Our money stories can be so overwhelming that we just tune out, turn off, and let someone else read the fine print. The actress Brooke Shields framed it well on an episode of NPR's podcast *Death, Sex & Money*. She told interviewer Anna Sale that she'd been meeting with accountants and lawyers, ever since her first TV appearance in 1966 for an Ivory Snow commercial. In all that time, she hadn't read or understood the financial or legal documents that shaped her entire life. She just handed them off to someone else. The jargon was overwhelming; deciphering it would take forever. Why not just let an expert handle it? Only when she turned fifty did Shields start reading contracts herself.

It's a great example of the kind of money story I hear all the time. Instead of seeing money as a clear path to freedom, choices, and security, we fear that it's tedious *and* terrifying.

We've been through enough already; we've worked ourselves to the bone—we're exhausted. It's time for someone else to take over. When you think about it, our money stories share the same DNA as fairy tales like *Sleeping Beauty, Snow White, Cinderella, Rapunzel*—take your pick.

Can You Help a Princess Out?

Think princesses are frilly, entitled little pixies? Think again. The truth is that all these princesses have a *rough* time. They're beautiful, sure, but they're also tough as hell. Horrifyingly discriminated against and abused by stepparents or evil, jealous godmothers, these young women all summon tremendous courage, resources, and the unlikely allies around them to survive and prevail, in spite of increasingly outrageous odds. Until one day, it all just becomes too much to handle. And they all simply shut down and go comatose until their heroes come to the rescue and solve the problems they'd been too maxed out to handle. And then they live happily ever after.

I bet most of us can relate to that narrative on some level. I mean, we know how these young women feel, right? We go through the *wringer*, we've done absolutely everything we could do to help ourselves and everyone around us—and now we're *tired*, for Chrissakes. Can someone give us a break, already? There're just a few things we need help with, jobs that will literally drive us over the edge if we try to deal with them on our own. How 'bout it, guys? Can you help a princess out? If you first need to go on a hunting expedition, a hero's quest, have a royal throw-down with your parents or prince, do it. Whatever you need to figure it out. But right now, we're just going to nap until you come back. Good night!

The prospect of having to manage our finances can induce a narcoleptic response in many of us, too. I call it a "money coma." I completely understand why we slip into them. But being in a money coma is dangerous. Your freedom and "sovereignty," your dreams and security, are in the balance. Lulling you into a deep daze, your money coma makes it seem totally okay to drop out of the game. It's not. When you're in that daze, you're going to make decisions that don't prioritize your highest good. They are going to come from a place of fear, desperation, or plain un-consciousness. Plus, staying in a money coma does not protect us. It leaves us vulnerable.

Face All That

I fell into a money coma, and my money story led me right to it. I told myself that to be successful I needed to spend. I told myself that I was good at making money, so if I wanted to spend more, I'd just make more. I told myself that I didn't need to save or invest because one day I'd be making so much money that it wouldn't matter. As I slipped into my money coma, I told myself that somehow things would all work out when I woke up. The last thing I wanted to do was wake up and face what *actually* con-stitutes financial security.

To be fair, who could blame me, a first-time home owner, for getting in over my head? No one told me. There were no warnings from the broker, the bank, or anyone else involved. But still, I had to live with the consequences, which were significant. I certainly felt like I *should* have known, that there *should* have been some warning from outside myself. The potential to blame myself was clearly there. I could have taken my financial disaster to mean that I was just another woman who was really bad at money. I could have thought that my situation was hopeless, that I should disengage. In some ways, I was set up to fail by my money story, and that story was fed by factors larger than myself, such as the social pressures to appear successful, to be a spender, and so on.

"Money touches every part of our lives," says New York–based financial therapist Amanda Clayman. "[Self-worth] or poor boundary issues, any sense of not being able to accurately tap into your own needs—all of this will express itself through money." Who wants to face all that? You may want to sink back into your comfy slumber. But your money story will just keep writing you into trouble while you're unconscious.

I've interacted with millions of women now, whether on a stage, in a class I've taught, or through DailyWorth's social community, and you know what? I believe that the only reason many of us finally face our money stories is because at some point we are forced to. Some trigger event detonates—a divorce, a financial crisis, a big life change—and we're faced with coping with the wreckage. We have no choice. We have to get it together, not just psychologically, but financially. We're not happy about it.

We feel victimized: *I don't understand it, someone else has to do this for me, I don't have the capacity, it's too hard, it means I'm not feminine,* and so on. But actually, we have the power to change our thinking—and our behavior. "Our money stories tell us something interesting and helpful, but that's not usually the full reality," says Clayman. "Letting go of that fantasy, or just being able to name it and see it clearly, that's a tremendously important piece of work. For some people, it's all they need to begin to change."

Rewriting the stories we've internalized isn't easy at first. But it's doable. Can we change the story so that managing money is enjoyable, interesting, and helpful in fulfilling dreams and wishes? It's transforming—and really worth it.

Pick a Fairy Tale

Everyone's money story is different, but there are common themes. Once you identify yours, you can start dismantling it to build a new one. You can even pick a fairy tale. Take Nisha's story, for example. Like *Snow White*, Nisha's life had revolved around beauty until she discovered in herself untapped bravery, industry, and compassion when she changed course and devoted herself to service and advocacy. But she still wanted to be feminine, and she still cared about beauty, and to her, that meant, "I don't deal with managing finances or investing—that's my man's job." She fell into a beautiful money coma and didn't take responsibility for whatever she was doing in the moment or what she had done in the past. She wanted to hold out for the big door prize; she deserved it. In fact, however, she was giving up her agency, the ability to direct her life.

Elle's money story was more like *Sleeping Beauty*. She sleepwalked through all her purchases and dealings with financial institutions—she wrote bad checks. It was all a dream anyway, right? But she woke up to painful encounters with her bank and her family. Rachel, a bit like *Cinderella*, believed that stuff—big purchases—would allow her to live with more confidence and personal power. Her big purchases would tell the world that she's got her act together, even if—she jokes—she is $1.8 million short of having enough to retire at seventy-five. (If reading this makes you squirm—I'm squirming with you.)

Today, Nisha has separated love and money. They are no longer conflated in her mind. Today she says, "I'm responsible financially. I'd like my partner to also be responsible financially, and whoever makes more money is inconsequential." More money doesn't mean less romance. "That's super liberating." As for Elle, she realized that when she woke up and faced reality—and money—she could make real choices about the life she wanted. It was a new approach not just to money, but also to life. And as Rachel comes face-to-face with her money stories, she's letting go of spending money as a way to feel invincible. "As I've started to reclaim my vulnerability I've found myself not wanting to wear that expensive motorcycle jacket I bought," she told me. "Which is a drag because it was freaking expensive!" Instead, she is starting to use saving and investing to support her existing identity (which is awesome, by the way).

Story Prompts

Your money story was probably written unconsciously, but you can rewrite it wide awake. That's the cool and amazing thing. You're not locked in. Money identities *can* shift without catastrophe. You can create healthy and positive money stories right now. You can pass them down to your children. The change can start with you. We just need to look at the thoughts and ideas that motivate us. In fact, your mental health hinges on your ability not just to find meaning in the things that happen to you, but also to integrate them into the ongoing story of your life.

Studies conducted at Northwestern University have shown that people who can interpret negative events in relatively positive terms—or describe what lessons they learned from struggles—tend to have higher self-esteem, an optimistic outlook, and a sense of being more in control of their lives and environment. Sometimes it's just a matter of brainwashing yourself—the way I did by telling myself that I was a "saver" every time I dropped a coin in my kitchen jar. They're called story prompts, little edits that you make to negative narratives in your mind to change your thinking. Research that the University of Virginia published in 2014 found that minority and low-income students at risk of dropping out—because they felt less intelligent and competent than their well-heeled white peers—made dramatic academic and social U-turns after watching "instructional" videos presenting evidence that many students enter college feeling that way, but almost always go on to succeed after a few months by working conscientiously, and not being afraid to make mistakes or to ask for extra help. The power of suggestion was all they needed to transform self-defeating "stories" into personal triumphs.

The same can be true for you. It's powerful to see what's been lurking behind your thoughts about money and what's been driving many of your financial decisions. Make sure your money story is working *for* you, not against you. But it takes a little effort.

Two Short Lists

I first got to work on understanding my money story by writing out two short lists, with an even shorter cause and effect bridge to join them. Let me explain. On the first, I jotted down the beliefs I used to have about myself to explain my behavior with money. Then, I identified the trigger event that caused these beliefs to change. On the second list, I wrote down what I now believe today and what actions I take to support my beliefs. It's a good exercise to start with—and I'll share mine with you.

What I Used to Believe—And Do—Before

- I'm a spender. It's who I am at my core. I like to give.
- My attempts to save money are always obliterated by unexpected expenses.
- I should have a big house and late-model car because someone as successful as I am should present herself that way.
- I need to spend money on clothes that will make me seem successful because if I don't, people won't take me seriously.
- No man will ever take care of me, so I have to do whatever it takes to succeed, even if that means spending money I don't have on my business to make it grow.

Trigger Event: Surprise Tax Bill and Home-Related Expenses

What I Believe—And Do—Now

- I'm a saver. I put my money away first. I *save* to spend.
- When money troubles hit, and they can still really hit hard, I can handle it because I have a safety net of savings and investments.

- People all around me take care of me—my family, my friends, my boyfriend, and even my investors. When I reach out for help, I find it.

Getting Clear on Your Story

So, let's get down to dirt. What do you really think about money? You may have thoughts and ideas that you've been telling yourself for so long that you forgot they were stories. You mistook them for truth. To begin, take out a fresh notebook or open a folder on your desktop. You can call it *money clarity*, because that's what you're going for: clarity around your money.

Getting clear on your story is about releasing shame and guilt. It's not about feeling horrible about the distance between where you are today and where you want to be. So it's against the rules that you spend a single moment feeling bad about yourself or your financial decisions. You're about to declare a new way of being with money that inspires you. Don't think. Just write what first comes to mind, quickly. You don't need to write in complete sentences; you can write your answers in a shorthand list. Let's dive in.

1. Evaluate the following questions. Again, don't think—just write whatever first strikes you.
- What's your earliest memory of money? Who had it? Who didn't have it? Where did it come from? **5–10 minutes**
- Were you raised in a saving or spending mentality? Explain. **1–5 minutes**
- Where do you think money should come from today (work, spouse, family, inheritance, investments, etc.)? **5 minutes**

- How confident do you feel with each of the following aspects of managing your money: saving, spending, investing, earning, and giving? Which one is strongest? Which one is weakest? Where do you want to learn more? **5 minutes**
- How much money do you think you have in relation to your friends and family? Do you have as much as you think you deserve? How does that make you feel? **5–10 minutes**

Pause and appreciate that you've had the courage to write down these ideas. Don't underestimate how hard it is to face your own beliefs, especially the ones that feel true but also don't serve you anymore.

2. Look at the messages you tell yourself about how you are with money.
- Write down as many things as you can think of that you often tell yourself about money in general, or your money specifically. **5–10 minutes**

Examples:
- ○ Money gives me choices.
- ○ Money is a source of power.
- ○ I can't earn enough to make ends meet.
- ○ I'm bad with money.
- ○ I have no idea where my money goes.
- Now look at your list and underline the negative beliefs you want to change. **5–10 minutes**

3. Now consider the following statements. Underline the ones you agree with; circle the ones that you disagree with.

- My partner/real estate/business is my backup plan, so I don't need to worry about money today or security in the long term.
- Managing money is someone else's job, not mine.
- I have bad luck with money. Only good luck will change my money situation.
- Managing money is something that men enjoy because it helps them accumulate power. Powerful men are attractive. I don't want to mess with that.
- I don't know what I'm doing with money and never will.
- I can't be spiritual and care about money—they're opposites.
- If I have money, people will think I'm greedy and cold-hearted. Instead, I should use any extra to help my kids/parents/friends/people in need.
- If I have a detailed budget and follow it strictly, money might work for me.
- If I can just stop spending, I'll have more money.
- The economy is bad, so no one can afford to pay me what I need or what my experience is worth.
- If I ask for a raise, I'll risk losing my job and alienating my boss.
- I'm happy if I have just enough. Having more than enough is selfish.
- *Add your own.*

Okay, let's take a break here and inhale deeply. You've just filled a couple of huge trash bags and tossed them out for good! Now let's continue.

4. Look again at your answers to question number three
   above. Identify one or two stories that interfere the most
   with your ability to see yourself as "good with money."
   Write them down in a full sentence so you're clear about
   what the story is.

- Add details if you feel inspired. For example, *Managing
  money is someone else's job, not mine* could become *I manage my
  money in collaboration with my partner/spouse/advisor as I learn
  how to do so more independently.* (Remember, this is not about
  beating yourself up! This is about looking, so that you can
  make meaningful changes.) **1–5 minutes**

- Then write freely about how true each one is—or how
  untrue. Don't stop yourself or censor yourself. Just go for it.
  5–10 minutes

5. Write down as many positive money ideas as you can—
   whatever speaks to you. *Bonus:* Create a handwritten
   or printed sign and post it near your computer. There's
   nothing more powerful than a reminder of "I'm good with
   money" when you're paying bills!

Here are some examples:
- Money is a force for good.
- The growth of my savings and investment accounts reflects
  how well I value myself.
- Money supports my values and ideals.
- Money is a spiritual expression.
- Saving money doesn't mean I'm selfish. By saving and in-
  vesting, I'm gifting comfort, ease, and security to my future
  self and not being a burden on my family.

- I'm good with money.
- I have the money I need to support me.
- My earning capacity is limitless.
- It's totally fine to ask for what I want and need.

Identify your money beliefs, affirm the good ones, release the outdated ones, and invent new ones. It's time to let go of anything you've believed that leaves you feeling shameful, incompetent, confused, or helpless. Studies show that spontaneously repeating your new, positive statements—and doing so often—can change your attitude and thus change your behavior. It takes some effort to get your neurons firing in a different pattern (I'm not kidding). But it is possible. There's no "hardwiring." It's all malleable.

Real, Live, Healthy

You may feel exhilarated to have a fresh perspective on your money. You may also feel slightly ill—like you now think things you didn't think before. Letting go of old assumptions and trying on new perspectives can be both exciting and somewhat challenging. Today is the day when you realize remaining angry at, or confused by, or disengaged from your finances will cause you more problems than embracing them. Float into the possibility of inventing new beliefs. Stop operating from your negative money story—and whatever unconsciously inherited social construct about your relationship to money was invented to frighten you and give up your agency.

Remember: money is freedom. Being in control of how we manage money allows us to design and live the lives we want. You don't have to master everything today (in fact, after this chapter, you might need to put this book down and go out for a walk). Just put your newfound positive money story on a shelf for a moment and take a deep breath. The most important thing you have just done is to replace your money fantasies with real, live, healthy realities.

You've just accomplished something amazing. Because you *are* worth it. Now let's move on to the main attraction: money itself.

CHAPTER 3

Grow Your Roots, Spread Your Wings.

Tether yourself to solid ground; set sail accordingly.

L isten. This is really important: it's very likely that you're focusing on the wrong things when it comes to your personal finances. I've seen and heard it in my workshops and talks over and over again, and it's the same phenomenon that financial surveys turn up in research over and over again. Here it is:

> Women tend to treat *budgeting and income as the most important aspects of managing their money.* It's not that these things are *unimportant.* But taking that view of life is sort of like studying the thready, knotted backside of a tapestry created by a master weaver, instead of turning it over and taking in its true artistry and greater meaning.

In other words, you don't see the big picture, much less grasp the depth of thinking and technique that go into producing something of lasting value—because you're caught up in busywork that's going to lead you nowhere in the long run. Why, *why*, do we *do* this?

It's not exactly our fault. For one, millennia of cultural mores have trained us to shy away from learning about the engines of commerce and macroeconomics, and instead to concern ourselves with the microcosm of home and, of course, our health and beauty. For another, even now, popular women's financial media still subtly reinforces that sexist mind-set. Blogs, magazines, digital media, and television cover ways to create, and stick to, various budget templates, as well as make changes that lead to more satisfying, lucrative careers. Coincidentally (or not), both topic and tone are strikingly similar to women's magazine–type stories about losing weight and fit living. Budgeting is, when you think about it, a lot like dieting (starting, and sticking to, one); the lucrative, creative career change theme shares the same DNA with guides on how to change one's mental and physical routines for a more energetic, fulfilling life. While both types of how-to can be helpful to a point, they both also encourage the same type of magical thinking about transformation.

Absent. Omitted.

To be blunt, no amount of advice on dieting or mindful living will ever really change the way you eat or think unless you are willing to confront hard internal realities. Similarly, financial austerity, or more income, won't lead you to lasting financial success until you spread out the facts and see what your entire hand looks like. After all, financial austerity on its own, like dieting, can restrict our sense of possibility and even the very ability to enjoy our lives; we become obsessed with the habit, rather than seeing other important pieces of the overall goal.

Furthermore, bigger income makes certain things easier, but it also creates new complexities—and ways to spend time and money. Don't get me wrong: you *do* need to earn what you're worth, and we'll get to that later on. But what I'm getting at is both simpler and deeper. And I've found that few women realize what really matters for developing and advancing our financial outlook and behavior—our lives.

What is important? So important that your entire financial security depends on it? No one is talking about it, so I'm going to level with you.

It isn't your budget or your income! It's not even how much you spend on average or the overall cost of your lifestyle. It's worth more to your bottom line than the value of your home. In fact, it's so significant that your entire financial security depends on it—not just in the near term but also throughout the course of your life. Here are the two golden words: *net worth*. Together, they form the golden key to your personal finances and to your long-term happiness. Burn them into your brain. But first, a point of clarification. The term *net worth* is used to describe so many different things now—from positive-thinking tropes like self-worth and gratitude to opaque definitions like *wherewithal* and *pecuniary resources*—that I want to be clear about how I figured it out myself, how I'm using it here, and how I want you to look at it in your own life.

When I launched DailyWorth, I couldn't find a single women's magazine, in print or online, that covered net worth in its financial advice section. I would read about budgeting styles, "rent vs. buy" calculators, or advice for changing careers or negotiating salaries—but no context for *why*. How did all these financial pieces fit together? There was no explanation of the greater plan. Absent. Omitted. How was I supposed to know what I was aiming for, ultimately? I eventually put it together myself. It comes down to your real overall value, what you're left with once you add up what you own and take away what you owe. *Net worth.* It's not about the short term: income and austerity alone. It's about the long term: roots and wings.

Measure Your Wingspan

You might remember my mother telling my punk tweenage self that to navigate life successfully, all I needed were roots and wings: foundational values and principles, as well as the confidence to take calculated risks so I could grow. I've thought about that metaphor a lot over the years and I've applied it to my life as a mother, as an entrepreneur, as a workshop leader, and more. I've also applied it to managing my money and funding my life on my own terms, and I want to urge you to do it, too.

Here's how I use the metaphor of "roots" in terms of your financial well-being. Roots are your foundational, principal assets. They are your long-term investments. They're your retirement accounts, real estate, stocks and bonds, maybe a successful business you own; in some cases art, jewelry, and other valuables. Roots grow slowly over time. They don't convert easily or quickly into cash for easy spending. They require regular, periodic attention, like watering, fertilizing, and weeding. Strong, long-term assets are key to your net worth *because* they are hard to uproot. And because they accrue value and compound earnings over time, they allow you to make money *on* your money.

When handled wisely, they provide security, like roots holding down a tree.

Wings represent your income and access to cash. How high or where you fly depends on how much you've got in your money market or savings account, as well as how you spend your money and how you use credit. You can measure your wingspan by the amount and regularity of your income stream, as well as the financial habits that you practice, and that affect your life, every day. When used wisely, your wings will help you bring back regular earnings and any lucky windfalls to nest above your roots, funding and protecting them. But wings will also give you the urge and confidence to take flight, with the freedom to soar and enjoy your life, in whatever direction you choose.

So, how do you assess your financial well-being in terms of the strength of your roots on the one hand, and your wings on the other? Ask yourself a few questions. Can short-term challenges or losses come and go without disrupting your basic stability or ultimate vision for how you want to live your life? If you've got enough cash on hand to cover emergencies, you can glide through financial surprises when they blow into your life because you've got strong wings.

When you picture yourself five, ten, fifteen, thirty years down the road, do you feel pretty secure because you know your assets are anchored and growing steadily? Then you know your roots are strong. But how do you measure how well your roots and wings are working together successfully? By checking in regularly with your net worth number. *Net worth*: get clear about your long game.

If you're like many Americans, you may believe that buying a home is an investment. Yet as we learned in 2008, a home is only an investment when the value of the house goes *up* during the time you own it. In terms of net worth, think about it this way: we usually say that you "own a house," but unless you paid cash, you really own a mortgage. When you reframe the transaction that way, you get that "buying a house" can have a *negative* effect on your net worth, at least in the beginning. You don't own the house; the bank does. You owe the bank.

Net worth matters because it's what you own in order to generate income when your career ends. Whether that's due to a temporary job loss or retirement, everyone knows that your debt payments don't stop just because your income does. If you have a positive net worth, you can create income. You have choices. If you have a negative net worth, you are penniless, no matter how much money you made at your peak. You have very few choices. Net worth is the only real measure of financial security.

I've Been Bad!

In this chapter, I'm going to give you an orientation to your net worth. Your roots and wings will help you fund your own dreams—what you really want from life—without putting your future financial security at risk. Focusing on knowing and improving your net worth is about moving from a micro mind-set to a macro view; from juggling parts to managing the whole; from debt and blind spending to knowing what you are aiming for in the biggest sense and taking steps toward that every day, no matter what happens. And here's the good news: the size of your net worth right now—whether it's positive or not—isn't as relevant as the direction you're moving in. You just need to keep moving in a positive direction. Do not slip into a money coma. Stay engaged.

I'll say this again because it's so important: building net worth is *not* about earning as much money as possible. Or, at least, it is not just about earning power. Making good money helps, yes, but if you're not able to save that money, earning more can actually get you into trouble. Radical, I know. For one thing, people are more comfortable thinking about income or real estate alone as indicators of their security and solvency. But for another, being rich doesn't solve anything, and it's definitely no guarantee of a positive net worth. Even women making $1 million a year (or more) can get into financial trouble if they're not using that income to build equity. Income is ephemeral. We know that the more people earn, the more they tend to spend. When they're not properly building assets—growing their roots—their wealth disappears along with the bill for their vacation home rental.

The same goes for making large "responsible" purchases. Buying a home, without balancing out how it works in your entire financial picture, might be more disaster than success. It definitely does not cement your net worth, let me tell you. Think about what I did. I put down too meager a down payment on a big house and took on too big a mortgage. The house needed much more work than I anticipated, it was expensive to maintain, and its value *depreciated*. Meanwhile, I was hemorrhaging my six-figure income paying huge bills. And what did I have to show for it, in the end? Negative net worth. And debt.

Debt is the other common obstacle to building your net worth. I don't mean simply having debt; most of us have at least some. But I do mean this: *If your debt is greater than your roots and your wings, your net worth is negative.* That's just a fact. Now, let's pause for a moment. Did your heart just stop reading that? Take a deep breath and look out for the thoughts that might come careening into your head. *I'm a hopeless case! I'm out of control! I've been bad!* Or *I should have at least been saving or investing sooner, and more seriously!* Stop it. Toss those negative notes to self onto the bonfire.

The truth is that figuring out how to build net worth is not tough. This is it: you build your net worth when your debts go down and your assets go up. When what you owe is less than what you own, you start to own equity. You are moving in the right direction. And moving in this direction is what you need to focus on.

Young, Unattached, Responsible Only for Herself

You now know that a high income or real estate doesn't guarantee stability—and that even significant debts aren't necessarily bad. You also know that you need to plant and nurture roots. They might not look like much to start. Give them time. Fund them steadily. Let those roots branch out. The value of your net worth depends on the health and growth of your assets.

Let's look at some numbers so you can see net worth in action. Take Hannah, for example. Hannah is in her twenties, has a college education, works in a downtown Seattle office, and owns a small home. Remember the basic equation: total assets (what you own) − total liabilities (what you owe) = net worth. Here is Hannah's net worth number:

ASSETS:	
Residence:	$500K
Emergency fund:	$2K
Retirement savings 401(k):	$30K
	= $532K

LIABILITIES:	
Mortgage:	$400K
Credit card debt:	$15K
Student loan:	$100K
	= $515K

Total Net Worth:	
$532K – $515K	= $17K

Hannah's net worth is positive. Granted, it is small relative to the investment she made in her home and education. But she will pay off her mortgage over time (which will decrease her debt), her college degree should produce better career income, and her 401(k) will grow decade over decade. Hannah has what we call "good debt." You use good debt to buy things that have a solid shot at appreciating in value over time, like a home or a college education. "Bad debt" is when you borrow money to buy things that will either decrease in value over time or get thrown away, like boats or Nerf guns. (I have a ten-year-old son. Stay with me.)

Hannah has a few things to watch out for, too. In the short

term, her emergency fund is on the low side. She needs to get it up to $10,000 as soon as possible. That's her safeguard against debt and curveballs, especially as a property owner, because unexpected expenses are the norm.

Long-term, Hannah needs to stay alert and keep tabs on all the variables that could affect her net worth down the line. Seattle and surrounding counties are beautiful *and* trendy, so real estate values can swing up and down, depending on location. Hannah should track the real estate market often enough to get a sense of how comparable homes are appreciating—or not. And hopefully, her home is in good shape, or the cost of maintaining it could offset its value. Hannah also needs to stay sharp on the job. If she doesn't make strategic career moves, her earning power might not translate into the income she'll need.

Finally, Hannah is young, unattached, responsible only for herself—perfect conditions for superspending. Like many single professional millennial women, maybe Hannah likes to travel as much as she can, try out new hot spots with friends at least once a week, splurge on clothes, drive a snappy car, and on and on. Her lifestyle could add to her credit card debt. It could sabotage paying off her monthly student loan payments. Her 401(k) could remain underfunded. Overwhelmed, Hannah could easily slip into a money coma early in her adult life.

No matter what age you are, however, growing net worth needs to happen intentionally and selectively. Otherwise, you're at risk of falling into a long Sleeping Beauty money coma, only to wake up years later to find your castle crumbling and your net worth in the red. So far as Hannah is concerned, she has a leg up on building solid net worth if she wakes up now and makes clear, conscious choices in her day-to-day living and long-term planning. The larger that positive number is, the more she knows she's headed in the right direction.

The Pumpkin That Squashed New York

Here's a more complex example. I'll tell you about my friend who earns a bank-load of money and owns a million-dollar apartment (but not really). Kate is thirty-five, lives in New York City, works in fashion, and makes $250,000 a year: total boss. She lives in her $1.2 million apartment (sweet) and takes two luxury vacations a year. She owns a Prius that she keeps in a garage during the week and drives upstate for weekends away with her fiancé.

Okay, so far she sounds pretty amazing—and she is. But let's break down what she owns and what she owes. Kate put 20 percent down on her $1.2 million apartment, so her mortgage is around $5,000 a month. Plus, she has to fork over more than $1,000 a month in co-op fees and building maintenance. And remember, Kate is in the New York fashion industry, and that means dressing like a runway model is a job requirement. Her clothes and accessories allowance runs $1,500 a month.

She has $60,000 in student loans and $40,000 in credit card debt sitting on her cards at 16 percent interest. The car costs $300 a month (*plus* the parking garage fee). Kate has very little savings—about $3,000 in her emergency savings account, which doesn't make a dent in her more than $15,000 monthly burn rate—and only $50K in her 401(k). So! Given this array of numbers, what exactly is her net worth? And what's working for her? Here's how Kate's numbers break down:

ASSETS:

Residence resale value:	$1.2M
401(k) balance:	$50K
Car resale value:	$28K
Emergency fund:	$3K
	= $1,281,000

LIABILITIES:

Mortgage:	$960k
Credit cards:	$40K
Student loans:	$60K
Car loan:	$18K
	= $1,078, 000

Total Net Worth:

$1,281,000 – $1,078,000	= $203,000K

Kate has a phenomenal income, apartment, and wardrobe—and a net worth that's appropriate for her age. But she's left herself very vulnerable. How? Her wings are like a hummingbird's, flapping vibrantly to keep her afloat. But barely. All her income goes into supporting her lifestyle and her residence. She has zero liquidity to fund her roots with any regularity. If she lost her job tomorrow, she couldn't make even a single mortgage payment. She's so strapped for cash by the end of every month that she can't make even a small ding in her credit card debt, so that liability just grows bigger and bigger with time—at a 16 percent annual interest rate. Kate is one of the rich in America living paycheck to paycheck.

Kate's roots are either stunted or not firmly planted. To have $50,000 in a 401(k) by age thirty-five—with no hopes of contributing more to it until she pays off her credit card debt—is not enough relative to her income. Kate's only safety net is her real estate, once she pays off the mortgage interest and builds equity. If the housing market drops, her asset deflates with it. True, the value of her apartment is likely to appreciate. It's New York City, where real estate is typically an excellent investment, so her plan might end up working. Still, it's risky to hedge such a big bet on real estate, especially when it's so costly to maintain.

So, didn't believe me when I said being rich doesn't solve anything? Even though she lives in a million-dollar apartment and has a big income, Kate doesn't have liquidity or equity. So, while her net worth looks pretty good on paper, her roots are thin. Kate shows all the signs of being in a Cinderella money coma. Her glamorous lifestyle and all its sparkly accoutrements could easily go *poof*! And those fabulous clothes wouldn't be able to help her. What if Kate lost her job and had to spend three months finding the next one? In that time, her credit card debt would likely double—and her savings would have vanished before you could say "monthly mortgage payment." She might even have to sell her apartment to shed those expenses, at a loss. There would be nothing glamorous about it. Kate needs to enforce austerity measures *now*, before the bell tolls for her—and her fairy-tale life turns into the pumpkin that squashed New York.

Freedom in the Making

On the other end of the spectrum, you might have a fair income and a modest lifestyle, but a solid net worth. Your roots and

wings are working for you. Say you're making the national
median income of about $75,000. By renting a practical apart-
ment, you're saving money that you might have spent on home
repairs and maintenance and putting it into investment accounts. You have $20,000 left in student loans, $4,000 in credit
card debt, $150,000 in your 401(k) that gets matching funds
from your employer, and a $36,000 IRA you rollover from a pre-
vious employer. You own a gently used car and have a healthy
emergency fund ($12,000).

Here's how your numbers break down:

ASSETS:

Active 401(k):	$150K
IRA rollover:	$36K
Emergency fund:	$12K
Car resale value:	$12K
	= $210K

LIABILTITIES:

Student loan:	$20K
Car loan:	$8K
Credit card:	$4K
	= $32K

Total Net Worth:

$210K – $32K	= $178K

In this scenario, while you earn almost one-third less than
Kate, your net worth is about the same, and you have access

to cash. You have strong roots and wings. You have diversified portfolios in your 401(k) and IRA. You rent to avoid repairs and maintenance in order to free up cash to fund your retirement. You're not living the fancy life of a high roller, but your net worth is solid, and you have cash in case you run into trouble.

This, my friends, is freedom in the making.

What She Really, Really Wants

You've got the scoop on net worth. Now, there's one more piece to consider. And it's by far the most powerful factor in determining whether or not you will create positive net worth. Ready? That piece is your *self-worth*. If you don't value yourself, you won't value caring for yourself, and you'll fall prey to every temptation to spend. And that would be a terrible waste.

The self-worth piece is actually really good news. Because there's nothing stopping you from choosing to value yourself. You don't need to get certified. No one has to approve you. You don't have to wait. No new muscles required. You just need to *choose*. Your mind is malleable. Declare that it's *worth it* to you to build your roots and wings. Then make choices that support that. Even today.

Defeatist or self-eviscerating thoughts become poisonous mini–money stories we tell ourselves about why it's impossible for us to succeed in our financial lives. It's not only untrue, but such roadblock thinking has actually been shown to *increase anxiety, decrease self-confidence*, and *fuel the sense of helplessness and doom*. The only antidote to countering this kind of anxious, paralyzing thinking and behavior, according to a Stanford study published in 2016[13], is to develop what researchers called "a learning mind-set": to "seek challenging tasks, know how to wrestle them into shape, and know how to see them through." In the study, they found that participants who were actively encouraged to think about what contributions they really wanted to make in life—as well as to take on hard work to improve their brains and abilities—took a test and decided to tackle 30 percent more math problems they'd originally considered too difficult than those who were *not* coached to adopt a learning mind-set.

The point? Dream big and act with courage. Don't stop before you've started by worrying that you've already screwed everything up—or that you will because you won't be able to figure out how to manage your money. Go ahead and be afraid. *Do it anyway*. Tackle what you've always thought was too tough to take on.

To me, the secret to valuing myself is no different from my drive to beat Kid Icarus, by being willing to hit reset. The same is true for you. You're going to make mistakes *because everybody makes mistakes*. So what? Reset. Figure out your mistakes and capitalize on them. And you *will* figure them out *because every idiot with even the slimmest handle on managing his money has figured them out over time*. And anyone who has figured out what she really, *really* wants in life, and knows that a little challenge is good, isn't scared or embarrassed to start again. Just remember: *The game is never really over.*

Double Bind

For some of us, it can take years to silence the obnoxious money story that says *It's not my problem* or *I can't possibly understand whatever it is you're talking about*—even though, as you've seen, net worth is not a complex idea. I can tell you everything I know, show you all my mistakes, how I am correcting them, and even so, you might struggle to move from spending to saving or from saving to investing. Beginning to build your net worth begins with *why*. In fact, the *why* can be where women resist or slip back into money comas.

But even if you're having trouble adapting to this idea—that claiming personal significance isn't counter to caring for others—you're in excellent company: it's the same one that female leaders in every field face, too. A 2013 report in the *Harvard Business Review* studied the subtle sexist binds that women face when they want to, or are asked to, step up and take charge.[14] Leaders in general are most effective, the study pointed out, when their work is in line with their own values *and* the collective good. This combination gives them a sense of vision, to see beyond workaday tasks to what is *possible*. Confident in their mission, they shed their personal doubts and concerns and take control.

But for women, researchers found, developing a mission-focused mind-set "involves a fundamental identity shift." *Why?* Because in most cultures, typically masculine traits are those prized in leadership—decisiveness, assertiveness, independence—whereas feminine traits are associated with subordination: being nice, caretaking, and selflessness. The disparity between conventionally "feminine" and "leadership" qualities, the report claimed, puts female leaders in a "double bind."

Sounds familiar. Remember Nisha, who felt that "sovereignty" over her financial life and being her own "boss" was akin to defeminizing herself? She's not alone. From business and political culture to mainstream and our own personal attitudes, the world sees it that way, too. As we explored in the introduction to this book, studies have shown that women who succeed in traditionally male fields might be seen as competent, but that costs them in popularity. Moreover, "leadership qualities" in men are perceived as confident and strong. In women, they're "arrogant" or "abrasive," and, as we saw, even "pathological," in Hillary Rodham Clinton's case. And that's just the first knot in the "double bind," the Harvard study observed.

The second? Female leaders who behave in conventionally feminine ways might be liked, but they're not respected: they seem "too emotional" to make hard decisions and "too soft" to be strong leaders. But the good news, the researchers found, was when women recognize this subtle and widespread bias in themselves and others, they feel empowered and can take action to counteract its effects.

Awareness. Consciousness. Wake up to the prejudices that you harbor about yourself, and you'll begin to snap out of your money coma. Free yourself from the double bind of sexism as you rewrite your money story, and you'll begin to shift the *core of your identity*. Hey, if Harvard says it can work, chances are it can work for you!

A Nervous Tic

But a lot of women feel so enmeshed in their money stories— no matter how sabotaging they are—that they just can't snap out of them. They don't translate the new information into the necessary supportive action. This is money story in action. It's the biggest threat to your financial security. And remember, culturally, we haven't been well set up to take care of ourselves financially and take pleasure in it. Instead, what I've seen is that women can be so oriented toward selflessness—to giving away our work, our input, our thought and care to other people *first* and for free—that when we prioritize helping ourselves it can feel selfish, stingy, or uncomfortable. Challenging the idea that women's work benefits everyone else *except* ourselves can take some getting used to. It might trigger a nervous tic in you.

Test out these ideas. Next time your sister asks to borrow money and you're strained, explain that you're "illiquid" right now. That doesn't mean you can't help her by listening. Ask her why she's in a bind, and what other ideas she has to solve her cash problem. Move the money you would have loaned to her into your emergency fund. Stressed about flying to your college friend's wedding? That doesn't sound like so much fun. Politely decline. Move that money into an investment account. In ten years, that money will take you both on a weekend trip to Jamaica—just you and her.

What does it feel like, thinking about denying family money they need, or missing your old friend's wedding over money? Can you imagine fully loving and caring for friends and family while also taking care of yourself? Ask: when you say no, what are you really afraid of?

Balance your priorities with others'. They are not mutually exclusive. Caring for others and attending significant life events can be some of life's greatest joys. I'm not saying don't help your close friends and family. I'm saying: balance your generosity by also caring for yourself, now and later. Know that you're a stronger and better mother, sister, daughter, friend, and provider when you have the strength and power of roots and wings behind you. When you fund yourself, you call the shots. You say no without apologizing, and you're loved just the same. When you decide to change jobs, you can afford to. You can make choices about what *you* want. And your money stress dissipates.

Still a Decision Maker

Listen, I know that it's hard to build a stable foundation when our default setting is to close our eyes, plug up our ears, and put paying bills at the bottom of our list of priorities—right under folding the clean laundry. Or emptying the dishwasher. Or cleaning out the car. But when you take care of yourself financially, you *are* taking care of everyone around you. Your kids have security, your parents don't worry about you, and if you need to make changes in your life, you can. With a solid financial foundation, you might even be in a position to truly help others if you choose to. Thomas Stanley, in his book *Millionaire Women Next Door*, found that millionaire women are much more generous than their male counterparts. Wouldn't it feel great to give, knowing that you can more than afford it?

At the same time, I won't lie. If you're not working outside the home—maybe you're raising children (or switching careers, or recovering from an injury, etc.)—your options for creating net worth are limited. But that doesn't mean you're completely screwed. True, if you're not making an income, you can't personally contribute to a retirement fund. But your spouse can open a "spousal IRA" for you and contribute to it on your behalf. And you can consolidate the retirement accounts you may have left at previous jobs. These are often referred to as "rollovers." You can manage joint assets such as your house: does it need repairs to maintain or increase its value? Or your retirement savings accounts: is your portfolio properly allocated and balanced? Just because you're not earning doesn't mean you can hand off your finances and go to sleep. Stay engaged. You are a decision maker. You have a stake in half of your household's worth. No money coma!

Calculate Your Worth

Now, when you first start, you're not necessarily going to go net worth positive today. Or tomorrow. On your way, you can dip further into the negative. I did in order to move from the big house into the tiny apartment. *That's okay.* I was course correcting. Investing in clear and longer-term expense reduction. Course correcting could mean shifting around, or even starting to build your assets (what you own), while preparing to more aggressively pay down your liabilities (what you owe). Sometimes course corrections take years to manifest. When I got divorced, I stopped being a home owner. That was significant. Becoming a renter, after living in a minicastle, felt dramatic. A big step down. A failure. I lost that huge asset, too. But the financial benefit was so much more significant that I dealt with my discomfort. Living much more modestly freed up my cash. It meant that I could start paying down my overwhelming debt and building retirement savings instead. Yes, it tanked my net worth for a while. But because I knew I was headed in the right direction, I didn't freak out. I knew I would never give up. I knew that in the long term, my net worth would rise. Like Pit. And I really, really valued that.

Over time, your net worth should go up. If you're decreasing debts and increasing savings and investments, you will move in the right direction. That's motivating. And you can compare your net worth year to year or month to month to track how well you're doing. Then adjust as necessary. Spent too much last year? Accruing too much credit card debt in the past few months? Not saving enough? You'll see that reflected in your number. So what exactly is *your* net worth? You can figure it out right now (and then we'll get into more detail later in the book).

To calculate your net worth, tally up your assets (what you own), subtract your loans and debt (what you owe), and find your number. Is it positive or negative?

ASSETS

Primary Home Market Value	$0
Cash Value	$0
Car Kelley Blue Book Value	$0
Retirement Accounts Value	$0
Investment Accounts Value	$0
Other	$0
TOTAL	**$0**

LOANS + DEBT

Mortgage Debt	$0
Car Loan Debt	$0
Credit Card Debt	$0
Home Equity Line of Credit	$0
Student Loan Debt	$0
Other Debt	$0
TOTAL	**$0**

You want your net worth to be positive. But if it's not, don't beat yourself up. That's counterproductive. Self-pity might as well mean setting some of your money on fire. Why? If you're wasting valuable time thinking about everything you've done wrong, you'll more likely disengage. If you disengage, you'll unconsciously hand over that $2,000 to your sister, and then book a $2,000 plane ticket to your friend's wedding. And WHAM, $4,000 in debt. So stay positive. Shame leads to unconscious reckless spending. Be kind to yourself and have patience.

Taking a good look at where you are now—clarity—is a major step unto itself. Just being present with your numbers, without judgment or regret, is a critical first step.

If your net worth is already positive, then what number should you be aiming for? To start, aim for that number to equal a year's gross pay. So, if you earn $80,000, your first goal can be to increase your net worth to $80,000. Once you've reached this starting goal, keep setting more.

Still not feeling confident you can do this? Financial advisor Jocelyn Black Hodes says that everyone's confidence goes through ups and downs, even when they've been awake to their money for some time. "As a financial advisor, I've occasionally been envious of my clients—not because of their wealth but because they were disciplined and determined enough to do all the right things that enabled them to accumulate their wealth and, in many cases, retire early," she told me. "Despite my expertise, I, like a lot of people, sometimes struggle not to do the *wrong* things that make being rich, let alone retiring at all, a pipe dream." So take heart. We're all dealing with our money stories, our insecurities, and the unpredictable nature of life. The most important thing you can do is stay in the game.

Net Worth Targets

These are not hard-and-fast rules—so if you're not close to these numbers, please refrain from feeling bad. These numbers are meant to give you a ballpark idea of what's possible.

	$50K income	$100K income	150K income
Age 25 net worth	$25K	$50K	$75K
Age 35 net worth	$250K	$500K	$750K
Age 45 net worth	$650K	$1.3M	$1.95M
Age 55 net worth	$850K	$1.7M	$2.55M

All. The. Time.

Let's be real: you can't predict the dynamics of your circumstances. My mom thought that if she married the right type of person, it would "work out." Instead she ended up a divorced single mother to three children. My friend Susie rose to the top of journalism, and then the advent of digital decimated her earnings. I bought a house in 2007 and it lost $200,000 in value in 2009. Then again, my grandparents bought a house for $90,000 in 1950 and lived in it until they died on comfortable pensions from their teaching plans.

Just knowing your net worth today, tomorrow, and next month won't prevent you from going through ups and downs. All. The. Time. Even when you think you're following the rules. But if your net worth is trending in the positive direction as much as possible, then you'll have more resilience to weather the major and minor dips. Things *are* going to ebb and flow. You may not feel like you're on track to hit your retirement goal yet—or not even close to getting yourself out of debt. But what's important is that you're doing things that build toward your long-term security. It may not mean that you have immediate cash flow or a fully funded IRA. But step by step, you'll put these things in place until excellent financial habits become second nature. Then you can wake up every day and affirm, *I am doing things to move my net worth in a positive direction.*

Fund That

Your net worth is about tending to your personal security. It's about owning equity that ideally grows in value over time. It means continuing to move in a positive direction, even when you have setbacks along the way. Because wealth—having money now and later—is not a magic Pegasus that descends from the sky. Financial security is not a windfall that saves you at exactly the right moment.

Self-worth creates net worth, and net worth supports self-worth. Believing your personal financial independence is worthwhile means you save and invest in yourself. Having modest yet achievable short- and long-term visions of your success inspires you to remain focused. While we can never predict what challenges life will throw our way, we can always aim to live the kind of life *we* want. It's not wrong. It's not selfish. It's not unfeminine. It's brave. And what's more, it's honest. So much more honest than the other options.

Own your worth. Live a life you designed. Fund *that*.

PART 2

Your Money:
Getting Clear to Set Yourself Free

Grow your money, feed your mind, expand your life.

CHAPTER 4

Know Yourself.

Who are you when it comes to money? Discover your
MoneyType *to make your best investments.*

ongratulations! You know what your money story is and
what's been unconsciously driving you until today. You
know what *net worth* is and why you should keep moving that
number in a positive direction, above all else. You know now
that your roots are your assets—investments that grow slowly
over time. You also might have a clearer picture of the kind of
life you want to fund and understand something about the incredible opportunity you have before you right now. That's a lot.
Now we're going to dig deeper into the dirt and talk specifics.

In this chapter, I want to help you determine which financial roots are best for you. I want to give you an overview of
the main options and then help you figure out which roots best
match your personality, outlook, and lifestyle. That is, the roots
that stabilize *you* might feel burdensome to someone else. It's
critical to choose the roots that you, personally, will be motivated to grow. With the right roots, you will want to have an
eyes-wide-open approach to your income. Now, you might be

saying, But my income funds my roots—shouldn't we start by talking about how much money I make? And how to budget? And what accounts I need? Roots come first. Roots come before wings: access to cash. If you don't know what you are going for, ultimately, then you won't be inspired to sharpen the focus on your day-to-day money habits. Your spending and your credit score just become another pile of "should-dos." Like, ugh. You can't quite get on top of them. And that feels bad.

So, instead of spending your paycheck on spontaneous pillows, lip gloss, alarm clocks, and travel mugs at Target—you *save money first* and feel rejuvenated by it. Because you have a reason to. You are funding *your* roots. You're stabilizing *your* future self. You're increasing *your self-worth*. You're saying, *I'll be able to handle whatever comes my way—whenever it comes*. Suddenly you see that your habits have a direct impact on *your net worth*. You realize you can adjust those habits to your great advantage. *You* have the power. *You* are in control. There's only one game to play: your life.

Relax About the Future

Let's review roots, for starters. By definition, roots are out of easy reach. You can't instantly turn them into cash to get yourself out of a bind or fund a passing impulse. When you're having trouble paying your credit card bills, you don't liquidate your investments. (At least not without a *ton* of soul-searching—and as a *very* last resort.) You will lose a significant portion of money if you convert them to cash. And your net worth could nosedive. If you fund them and allow them to grow, however, roots make long-term money for you (ideally) so you can relax about the future. And they slowly and steadily increase your net worth. Sounds good, right? So let's look at each major root option, one by one, so you get an overview. After, you'll get to think about which root, or roots, are the best matches for what I call your MoneyType, the way you personally approach life and money.

Retirement Savings Account, Part 1: The ABCs of 401(k)s

In the United States, there are two primary kinds of retirement savings accounts, and you've probably heard of both of them: the 401(k) and the individual retirement account (IRA). We'll go into more detail in the next chapter. If you work for a company that offers employees the opportunity to direct deposit a percentage of their paychecks into a retirement account, that account is by and large called a 401(k). If you work for a nonprofit, it's called a 403(b). You decide on how much pretax money you want your company to deposit directly into your 401(k) or 403(b), and boom! It's automated. You barely notice the money is missing from your paycheck. And you save on personal income taxes. Win-win.

Note: until you explicitly opt in to the funds your 401(k) is invested in, your investments may reside in a cash account. This means it won't grow. I've met too many women over the years who believe they've been investing in their employer-sponsored accounts, only to discover their money wasn't growing via investments. Don't let this be you! ARGH. You want to make sure that your funds are *invested* inside of your retirement account, in specific *funds*.

Sit down with the 401(k) manager at your company to make sure that your money is invested in *investment funds*. There are many different types of these—mutual funds, exchange-traded funds (ETFs), and so on—so it pays to make time for a formal meeting and ask everything you can possibly think of, and then go on to ask if there are questions that you haven't asked. There are no stupid questions. Again: there are no stupid questions. This is *your money*.

Retirement Savings Account, Part 2: Meet IRA

If you can't invest for retirement via an employer, you can open an Independent Retirement Account. Note: IRAs are not investments unto themselves. They are a type of account with specific tax benefits and rules. To begin, you can choose between a traditional and a Roth. If you qualify for a Roth, your deposits come out of your post-tax income, which means you don't pay taxes when you withdraw the money after you're retired. That can mean MORE money when you're age sixty-five-plus. Your older self will thank you.

Before you fund your IRA, whether traditional or Roth, learn the rules. There's far more than I want to print in this book because your eyes would glaze over. Regardless, here's one example to pique your interest.

You're allowed to have multiple IRAs, but in 2017 you're only allowed to contribute a maximum of $5,500 across all your traditional and Roth IRAs. That's $458.33 per month. So if you mistakenly contribute $2,000 more than the limit, the IRS will fine you 6 percent or $120 each year until you withdraw the funds and file an amended return.

There's also the SEP-IRA, or a "simplified employee pension," for small business owners. If you're the only employee, SEPs have one of the highest contribution limits of all IRAs. If you have employees, you put in for yourself *and* all employees who have worked for you for three of the past five years. There is also the Solo 401(k) or a Self-Employed 401(k). It's a 401(k) with a profit-sharing plan. That means your business, as well as your personal contributions, can contribute a percentage of its earnings.

Adjust the Mix

As you get older, you'll want to adjust the mix of funds in your 401(k) or IRA. This is called asset allocation, and rebalancing is the process by which you change the allocation.

Almost everyone should have a 401(k) or an IRA. There are only two instances when you should not start investing in a retirement account, or when you should put your retirement savings on hold.

The first is when you're carrying a large balance on credit cards at more than 5 percent interest. Why? If you have $1,000 in credit card debt that you can't pay off and you're paying 16 percent interest, you'll pay $160 in interest that year. If you were to invest that same $1,000 into your retirement account, at 5 percent average growth, you'd earn $50, which is canceled out by the credit card interest fees. Pay the credit card first, and maintain your cash savings so that you don't fall back into a debt hole, before you invest for retirement.

The second is when your emergency fund drops below one month's worth of expenses. Most personal finance experts recommend three to six months saved before you contribute to your retirement account. But I've observed that for many people, saving can feel like a hamster wheel to nowhere. I recommend saving one month of expenses and then dividing your savings between your emergency fund and your retirement account so that you experience progress. Progress is inspiring. Inspiration makes it so much easier to pay attention. Paying attention means you'll save and invest more. I can see your older self smiling back at you. She's very proud of you.

Investing: Slow is *Good*

Investing in the stock market is one of the simplest ways to build long-term roots—as long as you focus on the long-term and diversify. Diversification means spreading your investments across many industries. Mutual and exchange-traded funds are diversified by definition—they usually represent hundreds of companies in the United States and overseas.

The simplest and least expensive way to invest is through index funds. Index funds are collections of stocks and bonds that can mirror every sector of the economy.

For example, the S&P 500 Index Fund represents five hundred of the largest companies in the United States. If Burlington Stores, currently the five-hundredth-largest public company in the US, were to swap places with Neiman Marcus group, the five-hundred-and-second-largest public company, the index fund would automatically sell shares in Burlington Stores and replace them with Neiman shares.

Index funds are designed to match the prices and yields of underlying indexes, plain and simple. A company isn't selected by opinions of individual, subjective fund managers, but stringent criteria of an index committee and based on market capitalization (i.e., the market value of the business in the stock market).

Active investing is when you, personally, open an account at, say, E*TRADE—and make your own picks. Back in the 1990s and early 2000s, zillions of civilian investors decided to quit their jobs to become "day traders," hoping to make zillions on the dot-com boom. We all know how that turned out. Not so well. In fact, very poorly.

As long as you're not looking for quick returns (especially in your retirement account), passive investing is a smart, low-cost way to invest. Right now, "ETFs," or exchange-traded funds, are popular. ETFs are index funds packaged in a slightly different wrapper. Remember, focus on long-term gains. The short term will give you motion sickness. Your account could lose 20 percent one day, but then gain 25 percent two months later. Better to keep your eye on the horizon rather than the daily ups and downs.

Historically, the market has always gone back up, though it takes time to rebound when it dips or crashes. When you do experience a major drop in value, *don't freak out.*

Do not pull your money out of the market, no matter how you feel.

Wait for it to go back up again.

If you are maxing out contributions to your retirement accounts every year (good for you!), then consider further investing (the kind without tax advantages). No matter what you are doing, you need to understand how investing works. Why? Because the funds in your 401(k) or IRA accounts are investment portfolios just like any other.

Real Estate: Down to the Side of the Street

Many of us want to own property. Since the Eisenhower era, owning a home has been tantamount to being *American*: a sure-bet investment and a sign of our grown-up-ness. Now, there are entire cable networks producing sparkly real estate "reality TV" shows—which are, in fact, fantasies designed to tantalize viewers into believing how magically rewarding their lives will become, once they've put the time and effort into investing in the perfect home. Is it true?

Real estate can be a great investment once you understand the costs associated with it. Owning property gives you tax breaks, provides a financial investment you can put your hands on, and locates and grounds you in a community. It can generate income, and it has the potential to increase in value over time. In fact, its value can go up as your mortgage payments go down. One day—when you're older and most need to cut your costs—you could live rent-free. Plus, real estate is a relatively easy root to understand: after all, you can look at it and live in it.

But like all investments, it's not a guaranteed moneymaker. Like all roots, real estate comes with costs (buying the property) and risks (uncertain returns). Compared to a retirement savings account, for example, its appreciation may be less. Also, a big, well-appointed house with beautiful landscaping could be far less valuable than a comparatively dumpy apartment, depending on where they're located—regionally, for one, but even down to the side of the street. That doesn't mean you shouldn't buy a house. You just need to be aware if you're purchasing it as an *asset*, or if its expense is a lifestyle choice. Never fear: we'll look more closely at the issues later and do the math on renting as well.

Your Own Business: The Riskiest Root

Perhaps the least obvious root is building a business. It's also—by far—the riskiest root. People go into businesses for all kinds of reasons. Some start them to get away from the nine-to-five grind. For others, it fulfills a passion: they want to offer a great service that others are willing to pay for. Some salivate over the eventual lucrative handoff such as a massive Silicon Valley sale or an IPO. Ideally—depending on how you build your business—you can sell it to someone for more than it earns. Many businesses have valuable assets in the form of signed contracts, original technology, a reputable brand, and other "intangibles." All these things can be worth something.

A business can earn you more money than what you would make as an employee. A business, as an entity, can become more valuable than the billable hourly services you provide. It can, over time, generate income well outside of an eight-hour workday. Plus, you can leave behind office politics forever, reinvent yourself as the kick-ass entrepreneur that you know you are, and have flexibility in your schedule. It can be incredibly exciting.

In running a business, the potential for incredible wealth exists. But so does the potential for debt and failure. After putting everything on the line—your savings; your credit; your blood, sweat, and tears—will you see a consistent six-figure income? There's only one answer: maybe. Maybe yes, maybe no. Running a business is not for everyone. It comes with a steep learning curve and enormous financial risk. For the first few years, you're hustling 24/7 to prove yourself in the market—to establish trust and credibility, build your network, engage prospects, and win sales. And you'll be doing all four things for a long time before you see revenues grow. You have to be able to stomach the roller-coaster ride to profitability—or sometimes just to having a regular paycheck. But if you're passionate, organized, and love adventure, building a profitable business could be a good root for you.

Who Are You?

Okay, now you have an overview of your major root options—and we'll get into the nitty-gritty of each in this part of the book. But to me, it doesn't make sense to dive into those specifics until you have a sense of *who you are*, and how you're likely to behave, as an investor. The roots you want to plant and grow should, in my view, be compatible with your personality, as well as the volume and types of risks you're comfortable handling.

We all want financial freedom and ease, but we are all different people. I'm freakishly able to stomach high-risk situations and opportunities—I've always been a thrill seeker. But others are not. Most of my immediate family members are lifelong executives. While they have no problem riding stock market ups and downs, they have no tolerance for debt or income risk. What about *you*?

For example, do you crave stability, a beautiful home, and deep community? If so, then home ownership makes sense. If you're not yet settled and could consider moving to a new city, then you will find more peace of mind in long-term investing—portfolios you can monitor from your smartphone. It comes down to knowing yourself. So you really want to know: *Who are you?*

The Five MoneyTypes

Working with Dr. Jennifer Leigh Selig, a depth psychologist in California, I've developed an easy way to see what roots might work for you, how much resilience you have, and what you can tolerate. MoneyType is a psychological assessment tool that tells you your gifts, strengths, and sabotage patterns with regard to money. There are five MoneyTypes: the Visionary, the Epicure, the Independent, the Producer, and the Nurturer. Everyone is a combination of all five types, with one or two at the forefront. Take the MoneyType assessment online at www.moneytype.me or continue reading to see what resonates. Which one sounds most like you?

The Visionary: Balance That Risk

Visionaries see money as a tool for self-expression and a means to follow their passion. If you are a Visionary, you are driven to do what you love for work and equally excited when what you're working on is a great success financially. While some Visionaries may be highly motivated by money, others are satisfied with having enough, as long as it means they can do their creative work in the world. These are people who thrive on work that lets them express their vision in the world and who see money as a symbol of success, proof that their ideas and achievements are valued. The Visionary might be the person others call on to come up with creative solutions to complex problems. They're always thinking about how to scale things up and may have multiple sources of revenue—they are most likely never doing just one thing.

Visionary, Know Thy Type: Visionaries love it when others recognize their worth and invest in their projects. Then again, without meaning to, Visionaries can take excessive risks, making them financially vulnerable. Visionaries fear dying with "all their books still inside them" or without "singing their song." At the same time, Visionaries encourage us to take chances and follow our own creative dreams.

Challenges for Visionaries: Risking everything for the future payoff instead of building methodically right now.

Motivating Question for Visionaries: Since you love making an impact, ask yourself, *What big dream can I fulfill by establishing roots?*

CRITICAL PATH FOR VISIONARIES
Make Your Safety Net
Since Visionaries are willing to take risks in order to live inspired lives, it's important for them to create their own safety net. Having short-term cash reserves is imperative for Visionaries who don't want to feel beholden to an employer or partner and need to know they have the support to make a change in course without disrupting their entire financial lives. Go through your expenses to figure out your baseline monthly costs, and then aim to save a safety net you feel comfortable with. Depending on your risk tolerance, this could mean three months or a year.

Read the Fine Print

Visionaries are delighted when investors and supporters validate their efforts. It can feel amazing to have someone want to invest in your idea, but it's crucial to read the fine print and do some due diligence before hopping into bed with any investors, regardless of how angelic they may seem. Visionaries need to kick the tires before putting pen to paper on an investment partnership or even a business credit card deal. In other words, make sure you know all the terms before you sign on. When presented with an opportunity, walk through it fully to understand the repercussions. If you're considering an investor or financing, map out what that looks like going forward, using professionals like attorneys or financial planners for help.

Don't Forget About Taxes

If you're working on the side and have a full-time gig, make sure you set aside savings for taxes so you don't have any surprise consequences for your creative work. Know what you'll owe and save for taxes on a regular basis. Don't just promise yourself you'll think about it later.

Balance Your Risk

All investing comes with some degree of risk, and it's important for Visionaries to understand the risks involved in their investments. If you're already taking on a lot of risk by being a freelancer or starting your own company, try to balance that risk on the investment side: think a diversified portfolio rather than snapping up a share of a friend's new restaurant. Take a global risk snapshot and see where you need to get a little more conservative to counter some of the exciting endeavors you have planned.

Suggested Roots for Visionaries: retirement account, owning a business

The Epicure: Feel Encouraged, Not Deprived

Epicures love money. They love spending it, primarily on material possessions, services, and experiences. They may even enjoy saving money, but usually with a spending goal in mind, because they live in the here and now when it comes to money. Epicures seek the good life, and like the finer things, however they define them. They pride themselves on their good taste and it's all about quality for these women. Epicures work hard for their money, which allows them to feel good about spending it, treating themselves and others well. They like to enjoy life with all five senses, and when they have money, they'll invite others along for the ride. Epicures can be overly generous with holiday or special occasion gifts. They might start side businesses or work overtime to afford experiences or luxury items that bring them joy—and pay extra attention to coordinating fashion and clothing.

Epicure, Know Thy Type: Epicures love investing in enjoyable experiences, services, and products. But they also fear losing their lifestyles or never having the lifestyles they want. Without meaning to, Epicures can fall into compulsive spending, compromising their financial futures. At the same time, Epicures show us that money is fun and can be used to treat ourselves to good things in life.

Challenges for Epicures: Delayed gratification is tough for Epicures, who typically want pleasure right now.

Motivating Question for Epicures: Since you love wealth and pleasure—owning beautiful things, being pampered and indulged—ask yourself, *How will these roots allow me to maintain my great lifestyle when I'm older?*

The Bigger Plan for Epicures

Focus On Conscious Spending Goals

Choose items and experiences you're dying for and save for them with a goals-based approach. Make sure to set both short-term and long-term goals, and focus your reward system in a way that makes you feel encouraged, not deprived. Short-term goals are those that are less than two years away, and longer-term goals can range from a couple of years away to a long-reach goal, like retirement. For example, don't skip your latte if it brightens your day, but do focus on staying out of Nordstrom until it's time to buy the bag you truly want.

Save Before You Spend

For Epicures who can't stop swiping (or tapping) their cards, it's a good idea to automate monthly savings and create an internal "paycheck"—pay yourself after you've allocated money to savings and fixed expenses, then allow yourself to spend comfortably from your discretionary allowance.

Go through your expenses for the past three to six months to get a good idea of what you're spending, and establish which expenses are "core expenses" or needs (rent or mortgage, utilities, car payments, groceries). Then look at your flexible spending on wants, like manicures, meals out, clothing, gym membership. Rank those wants in order of importance to you, and hold on to that list.

Rethink Your Priorities

Be mindful of debt financing. Whether you're trying to keep up with a coworker or just treating yourself, it's easy to supplement your income with credit cards. If you've already built up debt, prioritize paying off the cards with the highest interest rates first. If you do purchase a home, proceed with caution. The cost of remodeling and decorating can wipe out your home equity.

Suggested Roots for Epicures: retirement account, real estate

The Nurturer: Putting Others First

Nurturers see money as a tool to help others, whether it's their partners, their children, their families, their coworkers, their employees, or their communities. If you're a Nurturer, relationships come first, and you'll keep others in mind when making financial decisions (even though sometimes you're aware putting others first may not be possible). Nurturers love giving and empowering others financially when they have money, and they follow the adage "time is money" and are generous with their time as well. In a relationship or family, being a good provider is a priority for them. If caring for others and nourishing relationships describes your main concerns, then you're a Nurturer. Real estate will be a very satisfying root for you, as well as retirement accounts. You just might have to remind yourself that when you save for your own retirement, you're better able to take care of others, too.

Nurturer, Know Thy Type: Nurturers love to provide materially for other people to make sure they are taken care of and safe, but they also fear letting people down and not having enough to support those they love. Without meaning to, Nurturers can invest too much money in supporting others, leaving their financial needs unmet. At the same time, Nurturers teach us altruism and the value of using money to love and protect others.

Challenges for Nurturers: Investing in yourself first and consistently.

Motivating Question for Nurturers: Since you love connection and caretaking, ask yourself, *How will my roots allow me to express my care and compassion for others?*

THE BIGGER PLAN FOR NURTURERS

Help Yourself First to Help Others More

Nurturers are exceptionally giving and kind, focusing their spending on their loved ones and cherished causes. Altruism is an incredible trait that we can all learn from, and money isn't just for investing in companies or belongings—it's a tool to invest in and support those you love. However, it's just as important to remember what flight attendants tell you when you're desperately texting and trying to shove your purse under your feet: put on your own oxygen mask before you assist others. This is especially crucial for Nurturers.

Don't Go Into Debt For Others

Compounding interest can work for you and against you. Don't use your credit cards to finance gifts for or loans to your loved ones. If you find yourself bailing out a lot of people, redefine what an emergency is and set clear boundaries.

Make Yourself A Priority to Keep Relationships Healthy

If you're a parent, make sure you've prioritized your retirement before you focus on funding your children's college fund. Your kids can get loans—not a dream, I know, but better than you sleeping on their couches when they're older. If you're in a relationship with someone who earns less than you, it's easy to be sweet and pay for more because, well, you have more. That's fine, assuming you're also funding your retirement and have savings.

Make A Support Budget

Nurturers can benefit from a goal-oriented plan that allows them to support people and causes they believe in without getting pulled underwater. Consciously carving out charitable donations for causes they believe in and setting goals and limits for gifts and support for loved ones can help Nurturers develop a "support budget." It's not about saying no, it's about supporting your own future so you can continue to help the people you love for years to come.

Suggested Roots for Nurturers: retirement accounts, real estate

The Independent: Too Many Rules

Independents deeply value freedom and autonomy. If you're an Independent, it's important to you to live life on your own terms and to have the freedom to follow your bliss. Independents tend not to think about money unless it's getting in the way of living life the way they want. They resist having money dictate their life choices, and their choices may not make sense to others around them. They may see money as a game with too many rules, and they rebel against how others say it must be played. Independents may have an easy-come-easy-go attitude about money, but that's because they are resourceful—they take a big-picture view, and trust they will figure it out.

If you don't subscribe to any system other than your own, resist the nine-to-five life, and have an easy-come-easy-go attitude to money, you could be an Independent. No real estate for you—especially if you don't want to be tied down. Retirement may not motivate you. But you love living exactly as you want to, so investing could be your best root. Maximize your income, and then maximize your growth. And maybe—maybe—own a business so that you're the one calling the shots.

Independent, Know Thy Type: Independents love investing in adventures and experiences. But they fear living in a way that's not authentically *them* or giving up who they are just to have more money. Without meaning to, Independents can fail to pay enough attention to money, creating avoidable financial hurdles. At the same time, Independents challenge us to rethink money's importance in the grand scheme of things.

Challenges for Independents: Connecting to the reality of money and its consequences—and its possibilities.

Motivating Question for Independents: Since you love freedom and autonomy, ask yourself, *How will these roots allow me to live life by my own terms, now and tomorrow?*

THE BIGGER PLAN FOR INDEPENDENTS
Rethink the Way You Think About Money
Delegating the detailed analysis and planning can be helpful for Independents, and it can alleviate some of the stress and anxiety involved in making financial choices and establishing a plan. Think about it this way: if you have savings and investments,

you can use the money to leverage even more freedom in your life. A former hedge-fund manager I know often referred to his savings cushion as "f—k-you money." As in, that cash gave him the ability to wake up each morning knowing he could tell his employer where to shove it without worrying about making his mortgage payment. If it helps, rename your savings fund accordingly.

Try an SRI

If investing feels too corporate and "too big to fail"–ish, consider socially responsible investing. Your portfolio can be screened to exclude stocks in companies that contradict your values.

Take One Step Toward A More Secure Future

Dreaming of traveling whenever you feel like it? In order to be whatever "you" that you dream of being in the future, you'll need to fund these excursions. Saving now and using tax deferral to your advantage can be the difference between having to keep working and being able to set sail later in life.

If you're self-employed, research (or hire a financial planner— we know you!) your best retirement plan. If you are employed by a company that offers a retirement plan, automate a substantive contribution.

Put It On Autopilot

Think big, set goals that inspire you, automate, and then go back to life. The more you can put your savings and spending, especially bill payments, on autopilot, the more time you'll have for the good stuff.

Suggested Roots for Independents: investments, business

The Producer: Structure and Control

Producers are grounded, diligent, and consistent when it comes to their money.

They enjoy accumulating it and watching it grow. They watch over their money closely, and evaluate their decisions about it methodically. Producers can be financially conservative; they prefer to minimize their exposure to risk, regardless of how much money they have. They're practical when it comes to money, and they'd rather save than spend on things they feel like they don't need or can do without. They are comfortable with budgets and financial plans, as they value structure and control.

If you are strategic and love to plan, you're likely a Producer. Spreadsheets and concrete goals make sense to you, so you can really get into most of the roots. Except for running a business: the uncertainty may fray your nerves. First, focus on building retirement savings, since it's the most methodical way to think about your long-term savings. Then you can get into real estate and investing. You might have a fairly good tolerance for risk, but too many curveballs will definitely stress you out.

Producer, Know Thy Type: Producers love to acquire, manage, and accumulate money, but they fear major losses of money or losing control of their money to someone else. Without meaning to, Producers may become compulsive savers and become overly conservative with money. At the same time, Producers teach us the value in planning for the future.

Challenges for Producers: Getting too rigid about what's possible or allowable.

Motivating Question for Producers: Since you love order and peace of mind, ask yourself, *Once I've reached my goals, how can I exceed them?*

THE BIGGER PLAN FOR PRODUCERS

Make More Than a Safety Net

Establishing healthy savings habits is a key to having a solid financial plan, and producers usually have the whole savings concept down cold. However, compounding can quickly turn on Producers when they're not careful. Get a good idea of how much of a safety net you truly need, then put the rest of your savings to work for you by building an investment portfolio. Walk through the past few months of your expenses to understand how much you need on a monthly basis to cover your bills and your basic wants. Then, depending on your job security and risk tolerance, you'll want to set aside a safety net of at least three months of expenses, or closer to a year if you're more comfortable with having a larger safety net.

Don't Lose Money (Thanks to Inflation)

Some Producers can focus too much on preserving and too little on growing and enjoying. A savings account is a precious commodity, but not if you're protecting it at the expense of credit card interest. While inflation might seem like a joke in today's economy, it's a true force, and if your money isn't working for you in an investment account and growing at a pace at least equal to inflation, you are losing money by saving too much in cash. After you've established a short-term savings fund, consider investing in a portfolio that reflects your time horizon, future goals, and risk tolerance. You don't need to go from ultraconservative to superaggressive; just work with a professional to understand where your portfolio should be.

Freelancers, Plan For Your Future

Producers usually kick ass with retirement savings, so if you're self-employed, make sure you've got a retirement plan that lets you max out tax-deferred growth. For example, an SEP might give you more room for contributions than a regular IRA. If you're employed with a company that has a retirement plan, double-check the funds you're invested in. Use your natural tendencies as a springboard to geek out on tax savings and retirement options to be sure you're truly making the most of your opportunities for long-term growth.

Suggested Roots for Producers: retirement accounts, real estate

When you take the MoneyType survey, your scores show you how each type manifests for you currently—it's called the "intensity preference." For example, like me, you may be 100 percent Visionary. But I'm also 62 percent Producer, which enables me to run my business. Some women may find themselves as extremes—small intensity around certain types, profound intensity around others. Others may find themselves blending evenly across several different types, with no strong preferences. If you've just read about all five MoneyTypes and thought, "They all sound a little like me," that's normal as well.

Already Full of Uncertainty

Not every root is right for every person. I've personally opted out of home ownership for now. I'm still recovering from buying the wrong house ten years ago. So for the past five years I've been building my businesses, paying down real estate and divorce debt, building savings, and funding my retirement.

Whichever roots you choose, get cozy with the idea that you can't know how your roots will grow. You'll do your homework, Google until your fingers bleed, call your brother, and say a prayer. But because of how the stock market, housing market, and business ventures go, there will always be surprises. It's *worth it* to weather the uncertainty. And in case you think uncertainty—otherwise known as risk—is always a negative thing, please allow me to reframe. Risk *only* means uncertainty. It isn't positive or negative. Risk just means that you cannot see the future, down or up.

How much uncertainty can you tolerate? It varies from person to person. And you may not know until you start to establish your roots. All roots need money up front to get started and more money to help them grow. For example, first you put a down payment on a house; then you repair and maintain it. You first open a 401(k); then you keep contributing regularly. How *much* will their value grow after you've put so much into them? It depends on multiple factors you can't predict. If you understand that markets go up and down, and that you're in it for the long game, then you're off to a good start.

If you think about it, your day-to-day life is already full of uncertainty. When you go to the grocery store, you need to decide where to put your money. Are you going to buy the large or small tin of olive oil? It's hard to know on the spot if the added cost for the larger tin will pay off, or if you're risking a hernia carrying the damn thing to your car. You have to make a quick call on the spot. That's risk. The good news is that a lot of people have studied all these roots for quite a long time. You don't have to blindly guess at what you're getting into. You make the best assessment you can and then start.

If you've been burned in real estate or in a recession—or know someone who has—you might be reluctant to think about establishing roots again. You might want to revert to Depression-era strategies, like Lisa Baughman's relatives in Cleveland, who hid money under the rug in their living room, in books, and inside furniture. When her grandmother died, Lisa and her mother found stashes all over the house. But keeping all your money in cash is *not* a surefire strategy for a secure future. If you have $1,000 saved today in a traditional savings account, over twenty years it's only worth $500. That's inflation: things get more expensive over time, so your cash loses value. Don't hide from risk, now that you know how to measure it. Build your roots back up again.

Start Somewhere

If you're feeling cautious due to lack of knowledge, listen up: *there are simple ways to begin building any root.* In college, I began experimenting with entrepreneurship. In 1999, I started my first e-commerce company called Y2Kgift. If you're not old enough to remember, 1999 was a frenzied year as we anticipated technological meltdown. Software programmers represented the four-digit year with only two digits, making the year 2000 indistinguishable from 1900. At midnight on December 31, 1999, we feared we would be sent back to the dark ages. Newspaper headlines touted apocalypse! Large corporations invested millions in reformatting all their software from two-digit to four-digit data capture. My contribution? I manufactured a "Y2K survival kit" that included candles, water, rice, and beans. I planned to sell them as gag gifts on Y2Kgift.com. In retrospect, this was an absurd idea for a business, but at age twenty, I thought it was brilliant.

I invested $2,000 of the money I made working part-time on Citibank's Y2K database upgrade project in manufacturing the gifts. I went to Chinatown and bought a huge sack of rice. I ordered candles by the case, printed sticker logos, and packaged one thousand kits. My mother was horrified. "You spent $2,000 on what?"

"Well, Mom," I told her, "It's cheaper than paying to get an MBA degree!" I didn't sell a single kit. But I learned how to program an e-commerce website from scratch, set up credit card transactions, and begin marketing a product. You need to start somewhere, and you will learn tons by experimenting. Don't get analysis paralysis. Just start something. Today, with so many free tools, you don't need to spend $2,000.

Deposit $500 in an IRA on a digital investing platform like Betterment, Aspiration, or DailyWorth's affiliate, WorthFM. They choose your mix of investment funds for you, designed for maximum diversification and low fees. Watch what happens. Starting small minimizes risk. It also gives you time to get used to putting your money somewhere other than your savings account. The biggest danger of all—the biggest risk to you by far—is doing nothing. Because inaction *is* a risk. Never engaging, never getting in the game, never seeing what's possible means risking our own financial well-being.

CHAPTER 5

Fund Your Future.

Support the life you want to live and the self you want to be.

Sitting at the kitchen table, I gaze at my kids, now age eight and ten years old. "Mommy is so good to you," I remind them, lowering two brownies as special midday offerings. "You'll be good to me when I get old, too, right? When I'm old and broke and have nowhere to go?" They eat in silence. I say this with exaggerated sarcasm. Even if my safety net dissolves, I'll do everything I can to avoid being a burden on them. But there's still a hint of truth in it, and I wonder, *would* they take care of me?

Nearly 50 percent of women still work past retirement age.[15] I picture myself at eighty-nine, wrinkled and hunched over. I'm pulling the soft-serve lever at Dairy Queen. It's like doing a bench press. My arthritic knuckles throb, and when no one's looking, I stick my hands in the freezer. Relief. Until a throng of customers tumbles in, a cacophony of children of all ages shouting out complicated orders all at the same time. My vision blurs. Somebody get my *blood pressure* medication!

At times like this, I get nostalgic for the old *Leave It to Beaver*

idea of retirement. Golly gee, it's all so easy! In the 1950s and
'60s, your husband was a company man with a steady career and
a guaranteed pension. Life after sixty-five was a leisurely pag-
eant of cruises, volunteer work, bridge clubs, and spoiling the
grandkids. I mean, seriously. That world—though first-wave
feminists rightly trounced it long ago—does sound desirable
versus the alternative, right?

There's no guaranteed security today. One in three Americans have saved *nothing* for retirement.[16] There are no "company
men" anymore—or women, for that matter. Over the last twenty
years, the number of times people have job-hopped in the first
five years after college graduation has nearly doubled. College
grads between 1986 and 1990 averaged more than one and a half
jobs, just five years out of college. Alumni of classes 2006–2010
averaged nearly *three*.[17] Pensions? They've been largely phased
out in favor of retirement savings plans like 401(k)s[18]—and
that's if you're even lucky enough to work at a company that
offers them. If you're among the more than one in three US
workers who are freelancers[19], you're on your own. And though
about one-fourth of American women now outearn their husbands, most US mothers are single and scraping to get by. *I'm*
divorced and self-employed. How am *I* going to afford to retire?
Kids—your thoughts? Their mouths are smeared with chocolate.

No Vacation for You!

I'll just say it: for women, the retirement picture looks pretty
grim on paper. Only 44 percent of working women contribute
to a retirement savings account, according to the US Department of Labor.[20] Women are almost 30 percent more likely

than men *not* to have retirement savings. Two-thirds of women (63 percent) say they have *no savings* or *less than $10,000* for retirement, compared with just over half (52 percent) of men. The gap widens as savings balances get higher. Whereas men and women are about as likely to have between $10,000 and $99,000 saved for retirement, men are twice as likely as women to have saved *$200,000 or more.*[21]

The big reasons women are behind, of course, are the gender pay gap and erratic full-time work patterns I talked about in the introduction to this book. Since women earn less than men on the dollar, whatever they do contribute is not enough: even with the substantial power of compound earnings, less equals less. And part-time jobs—which a lot of women take on while they're raising families or caring for elderly parents—often don't offer retirement savings plans—just 49 percent do, compared with 79 percent for full-time employees.[22]

At the same time, however, women have far greater retirement savings needs than men. For one, women have a different idea of retiring than men do. For us, retirement is *not* one long golf vacation. Where men envision retirement as freedom from work, women see it as working *less*, while *continuing* to take care of family, friends, and social responsibilities.[23] For another, women live longer, and our medical costs are greater as we age.[24] To be blunt, the current retirement system simply isn't set up for us.

Designed in the early 1900s, pensions, social security, and 401(k)s used to be rights guaranteed through employers and unions, observed economist Teresa Ghilarducci in a 2016 *New York Times* piece.[25] But the government hasn't kept pace with American lives. By 2020, the youngest of the Baby Boomers will reach retirement age, and Ghilarducci's prediction is that the number of very poor older people will rise dramatically. Social security and services will be strained. The middle class is already stretched thin, accruing more debt and earning less as the cost of living rises. The typical household net worth has *already* decreased by a whopping 36 percent between 2003 and 2013, according to a report in the *Times*.[26] Yet we may need $1 to $2 million—or more—to maintain our current lifestyles beyond age sixty-five. Studies show that a lot of women fear being destitute in old age.[27] We worry about running out of money or even becoming homeless after retirement. We have good reasons.

Good At It

But here's the good news. Since the recession of 2008, women who *are* interested in understanding their finances have been engaging much more with retirement savings. DailyWorth data shows that 80 percent of our readers (i.e., women) are actually in charge of household retirement plans, and 63 percent invest in a 401(k). No head-in-the-sand syndrome there. Other research shows that once women are engaged, they are no more risk averse than men. In fact, women actually save more than men. Let me say this again so you really hear it: women are not less qualified to understand what's in their retirement savings accounts or how those accounts work. In fact, when women do invest, they are good at it.[28] In a 2016 study, Fidelity found that of twelve million investors, women consistently outsaved men for retirement by percentage of salary—though their net was less because they *earned* less. What they *did* invest, however, outperformed men's investments.

But most women have yet to feel comfortable investing. In a 2015 DailyWorth survey we found that only 12 percent of women are happy with how their money is invested now.[29] A huge percentage (82 percent) admit that they know very little about investing (Fidelity's study put it at 90 percent). But they want to. Women know they don't know enough. They want to engage. And—you know what I'm going to say—they *can*. *We* can. We can end the decades of hiding and shame, anger and frustration (money stories!). None of us has to go through what Janice has. Take a look at how saving for retirement can play out in real life.

What Questions to Ask

Janice grew up in a rural community of Scandinavian immigrants in northern Wisconsin. Encouraged by her mother to leave their farming community and make a career for herself, Janice got a BA and taught school. She worked her way into the middle class, got married, had children, and went on to do much better than she'd ever imagined possible. She put herself through graduate school in the 1970s as a divorced single mother of three kids. She eventually earned a PhD and became a tenured professor. *Wow*. But like her family of origin, Janice never had a lot of money. Her day-to-day expenses and responsibilities (*three kids*) were overwhelming. So she wasn't focusing on maximizing her contributions to her retirement fund. Or making sure that her retirement investments were properly allocated according to her age. Her only direct experience with retirement savings was with the social security her parents and grandparents collected and the state teacher retirement plan pensions she earned while working in the public schools. 401(k)s and investments in the stock market were never part of her family's reality. Even retirement planning was a never concept to that generation—so there was no knowledge transfer.

Fast-forward to retirement age. At sixty-three, as Janice prepared to step down from academia, she discovered that the retirement plans to which she'd been contributing across five academic positions in three states were far, *far* lower than she expected. They hadn't been rebalanced out of equities into bond funds. So her investments, which were in higher-risk equity funds, dropped dramatically due to *two* market crashes: the 2001 dot-com bubble burst and the 2009 housing market fiasco. So instead of retiring with $300,000 that she believed she had, she had just over $90,000. That translated to $700 per month.

Like many of her female colleagues, Janice hadn't been tracking her employer-sponsored 401(k) plan. She had assumed that her contributions would be protected, as they had been in the Oregon system where she taught for six years. She wasn't clear on how this system worked and got poor guidance from her fund managers. "The advice I received was inadequate and inappropriate for my situation," Janice says today, at last understanding how she ended up in her situation. "I'm a first-generation professional. I'd never known anyone involved in investing or retirement accounts. I lacked the knowledge of these kinds of decisions. I didn't have enough information. I didn't even know what questions to ask."

So, after a very successful career—and a lot of scrimping, saving, and hard work—Janice has to get by on an extremely strict budget. Seventy years old and living in California, she travels when she can afford to (her pleasure in life) and prays that her rent doesn't go up. What should have been her moment to relax, travel, and enjoy time with her grandkids has become a time of penny-pinching and soul-searching. Janice barely has enough to live on.

I Don't Know

Janice's story is heartbreaking. But if she'd known a handful of basics, she could have made the necessary course corrections in time. The bad advice she got—advice inappropriate to her age and early retirement plans—left her in a precarious situation in her older years. Yet Janice's story is very common. It is the story of many, many, *many* women. We *think* we're invested, but we don't know how to assess our investments. We look for help, but we can't vet *who* is helping us. We either think financial advisors have our best interests at heart because they're the professionals, or we don't trust them at all. We ignore real opportunities and we ignore when our gut is telling us something is *wrong*. We're afraid to say, "I don't know." But allowing ourselves to be vulnerable enough to ask even what seem like the most basic questions—and to ask for clarification to make sure we *really* get it—turns out to be our chief asset as our own personal finance managers.

In 2016, researchers at business strategy consulting firm Advanced Competitive Strategies surveyed business executives, consultants, professors, and students to find out if people's mind-sets influenced their accuracy in solving strategic business problems. After each person answered the same straightforward financial problem, researchers were able to divide the group into four "types" of thinkers by assessing the way participants explained their solutions. Here's how the four types were described: 1) very confident, slow deciders (characterized by the statement *Now I know*); 2) very confident and fast (*I already know*); 3) unsure and fast (*I guessed*); and 4) unsure and slow (*I don't know*).

In one instance, about thirty male managers from the same faltering company—all with decades of business experience—all but snickered at the problem. It was ridiculous; the answer was obvious. But when they applied their obvious answer in a role-playing scenario against competitors, it failed consistently. Oops. Researchers found that the *I already knows*, confident in their snap responses, and the *Now I knows*, confident after pondering, tended to be older men and scored poorly. Unsure of their careful thinking, the *I don't knows* were overwhelmingly women—who consistently chose the best-performing strategies.

"It's not that the managers didn't care or were incompetent; it's that they were overconfident. When you think you know the answer, you sincerely believe it's a waste of time to keep looking for it," the report's author observed in the *Harvard Business Review*.[30] "I think the essential lesson for competitive-strategy decision makers is *not so fast*, in both senses of the phrase: take your time and don't be so sure . . . The willingness to apply that mind-set is what separates the good decision makers from the bad."

Do It All the Time

Encouraging, right? Bring a critical eye to your retirement investing. Ask for a complete list of funds that make up your retirement account. If the answer doesn't make sense, ask more questions. Who cares what the retirement manager at your company, your financial planner—or your spouse, for that matter— thinks? A learning mind-set, as we've seen from several different studies now, is the key to agile thinking, innovative problem solving, and acquiring new skills. So, again, don't fall into a money coma when it comes to planning your retirement because you don't think you know enough. Your self-questioning is the very quality that leads to better decision making.

For example, if you already have a 401(k), it's time to get really curious about what it's invested in. What funds do you own? How much is in equities versus bond funds? How much do they cost you in fees? What additional fees are deducted from the funds themselves, and are there less expensive fund options? Keep asking questions until you get the real numbers. A website called Blooom.com will tell you.

Also look out for your orphaned 401(k)s—accounts you've left behind at jobs when you left. Consolidate them under a single brokerage like Fidelity, Vanguard, or Schwab; a registered investment advisor; or a digital platform like Betterment, WorthFM, or Wealthfront. There are *trillions* of dollars' worth of orphaned 401(k)s in the US. A proper allocation with reduced fees could boost your investment accounts by tens of thousands or hundreds of thousands of dollars.

If you're brand-new to saving for retirement and don't have a 401(k), your best bet could be to start with a digital investing platform like Betterment, Aspiration, or our service, WorthFM. These are called robo-advisors (they're automated) and let you get started with small contributions of $50 to $500. Because they're run on algorithms, you can dig down into what you're invested in and how it works.

Magical Thinking

But at the same time, be careful not to convince yourself to rely on retirement solutions that you believe will materialize in the future—but haven't yet. All too often, we rely on what psychologists call magical thinking. Have a lucky charm? Consult your horoscope? Think that dreams contain messages? Cool. You're definitely not alone! Niels Bohr, father of quantum physics, built the original atomic model based on a vision he'd dreamed of. But here's the thing: Bohr tested his model when he was conscious, and it worked. That usually doesn't happen. When you believe that certain cause-and-effect relationships exist that cannot be *logically* connected, that's magical thinking. Even the canniest people can fall for it, especially those counting on an inheritance, according to an HSBC study.[31] Evidently, the mere *belief* that an inheritance was coming was often enough to convince people that they were financially set up to live happily ever after in retirement. In fact, most predicted that the incoming money would fill in gaps in their existing retirement funds (66 percent). And more than a quarter (27 percent) were counting on the presumed windfall to cover their retirement mostly, or even completely, according to the study.

Here's the fact: inheritances don't always materialize. Actually, they *usually* don't. Less than a third of those counting on an inheritance have actually received one, the study found. The major reason is that because people live longer now, they need more money. Your parents could very well outlive their promise to bequeath it to you. In fact, even though three-quarters *plan* to leave an inheritance, less than a third could absolutely guarantee one, the HSBC survey reported. Even if your inheritance comes through, proceed with caution. Like winning the lottery, once you have that chunk of inheritance money, you better have a plan for it, or else watch it slip through your fingers like fool's gold, as finance educator Barbara Stanny experienced when her husband gambled away most of her inheritance.

Even if you don't plan to inherit, keep close tabs on your mind when it drifts into magical retirement thinking mode. You might be planning to move to a retirement community in a more affordable city or country. In Costa Rica or Colombia, for example, the cost of living is very low and quality of life is high. You could live on $10,000 a year and have access to excellent health care, not to mention great weather. But an unexpected illness or medical condition could nix those plans. Or you might be planning to live with your adult kids—only to find that their spouses' parents had the same thought. Don't count on a future solution that's too fuzzy to predict.

How It Works

For most of us, the money we need to retire is going to come in the form of investing a portion of what we are earning now. (Do you really want to *have* to be working at seventy, seventy-five, eighty?) We put our money in—up to a maximum amount each year—and then when we get to retirement age (59½ and up), we begin to withdraw "distributions." That's how it works. How much should you save? Some say you want to have about ten times your annual salary put away for retirement. So if you currently earn the national median of $75,000, you want to have a *minimum* of $750,000 put away.

But to me, that suggestion is low. Remember, due to inflation, money loses value over time. That means that if you save $500,000, in thirty years it will only be worth $205,000. It will lose more than half of its original value. For this reason, investing is superimportant. If you invest money instead of merely saving it, it will grow in value over time. It even has a good chance of not only outpacing inflation, *but also* making even more money for you. Depending on how much the market goes up and down, that $500,000, invested, has the potential to triple in value over thirty years to $1.5 million. This is why you really, really want to make sure that your long-term savings outrun inflation. Since inflation averages 3 percent per year, your long-term savings need to return at least 3 percent per year. Ideally, more.

Your Number

So, what does that all come down to? You need to set a goal for retirement, and that goal should be your "number"—specifically, how much money you need to save to retire. Warning: if you've never looked at your retirement number, it will probably be bigger than you think. Seeing it for the first time can be downright scary, even absurd. But you need a place to start. Luckily, there are *tons* of free retirement calculators online. I've searched high and low for the simplest one, and I like the one at www .smartasset.com, but most retirement calculators will ask you the same basic questions.

Let's start now to get a sense of your big-picture number.

How much income will you want to live on when you retire?
$30K a year? $75K a year? (The calculator will adjust the amount for its future value.)

How many years until you retire? If you're forty now, and you'd
like to retire at seventy, the answer is thirty.

How long will you live in retirement? Obviously, you have no
idea, but for the sake of planning, say twenty-five or thirty
years.

Inflation: This calculator defaults it to 0. I recommend you
make it 3 percent.

Annual yield on balance? It's defaulted to 7.5 percent. To be
conservative, make it 5 percent.

After finding out your number, write down the figure here:

_____.

Regular People

Remember, this is a goal. It's just a north star to orient yourself.
It's not a measure of your intrinsic worth or a statement about
how responsible you are. Never thought of yourself as a millionaire wannabe? Stop looking at that big number. The number is
your ultimate goal: you may not get there for a while. My goal is
$2 million. I'm thirty-nine and not a third of the way there yet
unless you count the market value of my businesses. But they
aren't liquid, so I won't count on them. Like Kid Icarus, I look at
it as a game, not a death sentence. Once you have a goal to aim
for, especially if you write it down, your behaviors and choices
will adjust.

If you're older, you can still make a dramatic change later
in life. My mom didn't even *start* saving for retirement until
she was forty-two, and she reached her goal to fully retire at
seventy-two. How? Once she was in the workforce, she max-

imized her 401(k) contributions and took advantage of every employee benefit program offered. She also educated herself on what to put in her portfolios. Today, in her seventies, she works with a fee-only financial advisor, but she directs the funds herself at Vanguard, a discount brokerage.

So, stay with me. If my mom can do it at forty-two in the 1980s with no assets from her divorce other than a house, so can you. Every $100 you stash away matters. The fifties and sixties are prime earning years. Your career is peaking. Your kids are growing up or already out of the house. You have more money available to put aside. Plus, the IRS allows people over fifty to put more money aside for retirement. As you engage, you will realize that making small regular contributions doesn't affect your cash flow that much. And that will add to your confidence, which has a snowball effect.

It turns out that millionaires are regular people. Stats show that they do not typically splurge on sapphire necklaces and fancy homes. They live modestly and prioritize saving over spending. According to a 2014 study from Spectrem Group, millionaires attribute their wealth to these top five reasons:

1. hard work
2. education
3. smart investing
4. living below their means
5. knowing when and how to take risks

You can do all these things, and will, including numbers four and five. Guess what? You're aiming to be a millionaire, too.

And you're going to do it. Once you have clarity, open up the accounts you need, if you haven't already, and set up automatic monthly transfers. Aim to contribute as much as you can to the appropriate retirement accounts and increase that contribution at least annually. The next step is choosing your investments within your retirement accounts. And you can start to learn about how to do that right now. Just turn the page.

CHAPTER 6

Go to Market.

*You don't need to learn stocks—you need to learn
how to invest according to a few basic guidelines.*

As a budding twenty-three-year-old entrepreneur, eager to make my way in the world and to make money, I invested $2,000 in specific stocks on E*TRADE. I had no idea what to buy, but my boyfriend at the time worked for Ford Motor Company. So I chose Ford. Then my stocks immediately went down in value. Like, a week later. I lost 30 percent of what I'd invested. Oops. But even worse—much worse, in fact—was the move I made next. I bailed. The real problem was not actually the $700 I lost. It was not understanding that I needed to stick around for the long term to make my investment work. In other words, I needed to keep my account open and not touch anything.

I blamed myself. I thought my loss meant I was bad at picking stocks. That was in fact true—I had no business picking stocks—but I didn't know there was any other way to invest. So I got out completely. Sold everything. Threw in the towel. Aargh. I basically sealed my fate. I should have waited for the market to go back up, which it did, as it usually does over time. I would have recouped the $700 and likely made more money. And then I would have experienced the thrill I was looking for—the thrill of making free money on my money.

Never Get Out Alive

Raise your hand if you've ever slipped into a money coma at the first mention of Wall Street gobbledygook like *asset class*, *diversification*, or *basis point*. I see many of yours are raised. So is mine. I used to feel ashamed that I didn't know what any of it meant. Even when I'd occasionally get inspired to learn, I'd check out an investment services website only to feel assaulted by stock tickers, mobs of graphs and charts with weird decimals, and positive and negative percentages corresponding to who knows what. Why spend what little free time I had trying to slash my way through *that* swamp? I'd never get out alive.

Women are twice as likely as men to feel like they don't know what to do with investments, according to research.[32] When it comes to bigger-picture finances—looking deeply into what funds are actually in their 401(k)s, or investing outside of retirement accounts—women can feel like they're doomed to mess things up. Men, however, are often so eager to call the shots that they'll make impulsive *I already know* investments even when they're just as confused as we are, as many studies show. We also know from those same studies that women don't want to put themselves, and definitely not their families, in any tight spots.

Many women feel this way. So we quit too soon. Hold too tightly to cash. Tuck it in a money market or savings account, where we know we can get it out when we want to and if we need to. This is true for women who have no 401(k) or IRA, and don't know what a brokerage firm is. It's also true for highly funded women who have so much money they could easily max out their retirement funds.

A healthy savings account is a must. But if you have strong wings—emergency savings and good liquidity—you *need* to do something else with the rest of your cash. You could end up making a measly half percent interest in a traditional savings account instead of—*cha-ching!*—sometimes 10 or 20 percent in good years in an investment account. Investing is a *huge* opportunity. You really don't want to miss out. You invest money, and, following a few basic principles, you make money. You can do it.

Psyche Yourself Out

The data is promising. As we've seen in studies, once women get over their crisis of confidence, they're really good at financial management *because* they're not resolute of their abilities to make good investment choices. Women's tendency to be more conservative, to think more collaboratively, and to seek expert advice really works well in navigating the market. So when the market goes up and down, they have a better chance of being less reactive and keeping their money invested instead of panicking and pulling it out. That's what we need for long-term gain.

Women can also be motivated by the idea of covering their long-term needs and those of their families and communities. Scholar Deborah Tannen observes that women tend to see the world as a web of networks, which tempers temptations to take rash action.[33] Rash action is no friend to profitable investing. Slow and steady engagement is what you want. It's not *just* about saving up to pay orthopedic surgeons in your seventies. It's about having plenty of money to cover ourselves well in the near future, and then moving on to do more interesting things. Again, my sisters, I'll pound out the same drumbeat so that you hear it loud and clear: the key to investing is *not to psyche yourself out of it.*

An Unabashed, Self-Aware Student

Consider the findings of Proteus International founding partner Erika Andersen, who advises the CEOs and top executives of corporations such as NBCUniversal, Facebook, Hyatt Hotels Corporation, GE, Hulu, Madison Square Garden, and more. In her more than thirty years of experience of management consulting, guess who Andersen and her colleagues have found to be the most successful business strategists and leaders? Those with "a willingness to experiment and become a novice again and again." In other words, humble, deliberate learners—specifically those who share the traits of aspiration, self-awareness, curiosity, and vulnerability. "They truly want to understand and master new skills; they see themselves very clearly; they constantly think of and ask good questions; and they tolerate their own mistakes as they move up the learning curve," Andersen reports.

Sounds awesome. How can *you* transform yourself into an unabashed, self-aware student—open to learning about, even getting really good at, investing? Andersen advises the same basic inner narrative editing technique we've seen in other studies to transform negative money stories. At heart, it's not unlike the Jedi mind trick I used to "brainwash" myself to change my self-perceived identity from "spender" to "saver." The idea is this. Whenever you catch yourself resistant to learn new stuff—*it's too complicated, someone else is better at it, I don't need to*—flip that internal voice on its head. Change your story.

Andersen offers a simple chart to help change your defeatist self-narrative into an optimistic one, in a 2016 *Harvard Business Review* article describing research in her book *Be Bad First: Get Good at Things FAST to Stay Ready for the Future.*[34]

Changing Your Inner Narrative

DON'T SAY THIS	SAY THIS
I don't need to learn this.	What would my future look like if I did?
I'm already fine at this.	Am I really? How do I compare with my peers?
This is boring.	I wonder why others find it interesting.
I'm terrible at this.	I'm making beginner mistakes but I'll get better.

Underline that last point—again. The willingness to say *I don't know* and to make novice mistakes in order to learn new skills is a major *asset* for women in investing. In fact, Stanford researchers found in the late 1980s that people who are urged to make mistakes early on in any learning process end up with "heightened interest, persistence, and better performance."[35] Wrap your head around *that.*

"Buy Low, Sell High"

Stop the presses. Turn off the Internet. Tune out the noise. Financial media will not help you get rich quick. It's designed to grip your attention and then sell ads to Schwab and Edward Jones. I fell for it. Investing in the stock market can be one of the simplest and lowest-risk ways to build long-term roots. The smart, low-cost way to invest is boring, low-cost, and quite mellow. It's called passive investing—though, as we'll see, it still requires your active attention.

The basic deal is this. There are two ways to invest: actively and passively. What I did when I lost money on E*TRADE was active investing. It's what professional investors do. It's what normal people do, too, and can do well when they understand the risk. **Active investing** means picking your own stocks, one by one, and investing your money in them directly, either online or through a broker. **Active funds** are made of the stocks and other assets that a professional portfolio manages, which means they are also usually more expensive in fees. Yahoo Finance and MarketWatch cater to active investors.

Active investors are in the game to beat the market growth. They're constantly checking their smartphones to see how their stocks are faring—hour by hour, minute to minute. It's a lot of work and *a lot* of stress. But some people love the challenge and the rush.

In active investing, the goal is to buy stock in companies you believe *will* grow in value.

Active investors, for example, are always on the lookout for promising companies that are poised to "go public," so they can "get in on the IPO." Translation: by joining the stock market, companies wanting to build enormous growth capital invite the public to purchase shares known as an initial public offering (IPO). Highly anticipated IPOs can cause buying frenzies (think back to the mad rush to buy Facebook stock, for example). Active investors' hope is to get in "at the ground floor," watch as that stock soars in value, and then sell it at its peak. Hence the old expression "buy low, sell high." But is it easy money?

Buy and Hold

Not so much. *Tons* of variables impact a stock's value at any given moment: competition, new technology, national and global politics, foreign markets, natural disasters, and on and on. At least 80 percent of people who try to beat the market—meaning, make a big profit—never do. The risk is very high. You may *never* transition to active investing or direct stock picking, and that's *fine*. If you do transition to active investing, only do so with money you can afford to lose.

Passive investing, on the other hand, is known as a "buy and hold" style of investing. Passive investing requires patience because the market ebbs and flows. It takes time. In fact, it's about as exciting "as watching paint dry," goes the famous quip of American economist Paul Samuelson. That's what you want. Either through a financial advisor, discount brokerage, or robo-advisor, you explore what's appropriate for your age (how long until you retire?), your risk tolerance, and the outcome you're looking for. And then you buy shares in the appropriate mix of index funds.

Passive funds include funds that mirror the financial indexes that track the value of various sectors of the economy, such as the Standard & Poor's 500 Index (S&P 500). These are called *index funds,* and their price goes up and down with their slice of the market. What does that mean? It means that if, for example, a stock has 5 percent of the S&P 500 Index (a collection of five hundred top-grossing American companies), it will represent 5 percent of the index fund. So, when the index goes up, your stock price goes up and you make money. When the index goes down, you lose money.

Because index funds track indexes, they don't require human analysis. Therefore, they cost less to manage. Investing in index funds gives average mortals like us a fighting chance of making money on our investments. They carry lower costs for consumers and fewer tax implications and require less maintenance than their high-touch, high-maintenance counterparts, mutual funds. **Mutual funds** allow individuals to invest passively in professionally managed funds made up of stocks and bonds chosen by expert analysts. But, again, because they're managed by humans, actively managed mutual funds carry costs that index funds don't.

Over the past eighty years, the stock market has returned, on average, 10 percent per year. However, returns on individual stocks vary widely. There's no guaranteeing what the market will do. For example, in 2008, the market dropped 50 percent, while in 2011 it was flat. In 2012 it returned about 13 percent, and in 2013 we recovered from 2008 (if you were still *in* the market, that is). This is what people mean when they talk about market fluctuation. And this is where your tolerance for risk comes in.

Investing Vocab in Plain English

Asset: A financial thing you own.

Stock: Ownership of a piece of a company.

Bond: A loan you make to a government or a company.

Words used interchangeably: Stock, share, equity.

Asset class: Categories of things you own, e.g., stocks, bonds, real assets (e.g., real estate).

Asset allocation: How your investments are distributed across asset classes. When done properly, your allocation factors in your age, income, and risk tolerance.

Risk: The chance that the returns on your investments will be different than you expected (positively or negatively).

Risk tolerance: How you might feel if your investments suddenly tank—even when you know they will eventually come back up.

Fund: A *mix* of stocks, bonds, and cash equivalents.

Types of funds: Mutual funds (broadest), index funds (less broad), exchange-traded funds (specific).

Brokerage: A company that helps buyers and sellers of investments to make transactions.

Portfolio: The collection of funds that *you* invest in.

Diversification: Owning several different kinds of assets. Helps minimize risk.

Index: A number that measures a sector of the economy. For example, the S&P 500 Index tracks five hundred large American companies. The NASDAQ tracks three thousand big tech and biotech companies.

Timing the Market: Buying or selling portions of your portfolio because you think the market is high or low. If you try to time the market, you're more likely to be wrong, so don't do it.

You Love Risk. No, Really.

Every year articles and papers are published on how women are more "risk averse" than men. But what the stats *actually* say is much more nuanced, according to a study published by the Institute for New Economic Thinking. The question does not appear to be whether women are more unwilling than men to make bold investment bets and decisions; rather, we consider the risks differently. Women tend to make fewer careless decisions than men, according to NASDAQ executive Adena Friedman: we should celebrate women's tendency to measure risk, examine possibilities, and calculate potential costs and benefits before plunging into new ventures.

Yet everyone has different perceptions of risk. It is an emotional judgment. Meaning, your perception of the risk in front of you is not an *actual* measure of risk. Risk means how much *you* can afford to lose, in your mind, in your nervous system, and still be able to sleep at night. It's the extreme that you *feel* you can afford to lose. Test it out: if you went to a casino and put $10,000 on the table, how would you feel if you lost that $10,000? How about if I told you that you *also* know that you have a 10 percent chance of winning $100,000. Now how do you feel about taking the risk?

I believe most women will do best when we get active in passive investing.

Encounter with a Finance Mogul

Let me tell you a story of my encounter with a well-established, ultrawealthy man who made his fortune through active investing. A friend had passed me a new book by the master finance mogul Martin Sosnoff. What could an old-school Wall Street financier want with me? Turns out, Sosnoff had read about Daily-Worth in *Forbes* and wanted to know if I would read his book and interview him.

Sosnoff is a successful money manager. As CEO of Atalanta Sosnoff Capital, LLC, he manages *$5 billion* in assets. He also collects provocative art and rides dressage horses. (I had no idea what those were.) Looking at the book cover, I assumed he was like most Wall Street money managers. They mock investors like me, thinking we play it too safe. Because we favor passive investing, we lose out on making serious money. Or so they think. I disagree. I believe strongly that passive investing is the smarter way to invest: the market grows decade over decade, and so will my money. It has nothing to do with risk aversion, gender, or lack of cojones.

In short, I wasn't sure about this Sosnoff meeting. Did I really want to schlep up to New York to get a condescending lecture from a Wall Street muckety-muck? But I'd heard about Sosnoff through colleagues and mentors. *Barron's* called him "a mix of hipster and iconoclast." I like hipsters and iconoclasts. So I cracked open the book. In the second chapter of *Master Class for Investors*, Sosnoff had written that money is a game every American citizen should play. Some of us grasp the game well enough to thrive. Most don't. I liked what I was reading. It jelled with my experiences at DailyWorth.

A few weeks later, he welcomed me into his Manhattan office. I don't get intimidated easily, but I admit it: I felt just a little bit intimidated. Okay, a lot. Here was one of the kings in a city of high rollers—and he'd written a book that I hadn't expected to admire but really, really did. I wanted him to take me seriously as a professional. All of a sudden, my outfit felt totally wrong. I triple-checked my hair and lip gloss in the elevator mirror on the way up. But Sosnoff, a natty dresser himself and a big personality, put me right at ease.

During our interview, Sosnoff said that he wanted to help less-savvy investors learn how the markets work. "I wrote this book for anyone who has at least ten thousand dollars to invest and wants to learn more about how financial markets function, how the markets respond to crises like 9/11, and what makes them so dysfunctional," he told me.

I decided to lay all my cards on the table. "Martin, I don't think most investors, people like me and those your book is aimed at, should make investing decisions around timing the market—active investing just doesn't yield great returns for most people," I argued. "I recommend passive investing, steady, regular contributions to investment accounts, and taking advantage of tax breaks." He agreed with me. I was confused. Martin Sosnoff agreed with me?

But he cautioned my confidence. He underscored that his most crucial life lesson also applied to investing: there's no map to follow. Understandable coming from a man raised in poverty who almost froze to death fighting in the Korean War. "Any investor, whether a professional working at it ten hours a day, or somebody who is disinterested in Wall Street's day-to-day mumbo-jumbo, should have a point of view on what's happening," he said. "Trusting anything or anyone—from a financial advisor to a passive investing strategy—is not an excuse to take your hands off the wheel."

Thanks, Martin. I left the interview still a resolute passive investor. But I heard him. It was a good reminder: Keep learning and stay awake. Always. And passive investing *isn't* an excuse to ignore how your money is invested. Learn about the S&P versus the MSCI. Grasp the basics of equities versus fixed income. The more you read and ask, the more it will all begin to click. You really *can* do it. Believe me!

Your Spread Protects You

So let's get down to the business of *how* to invest passively. You already know about the types of *accounts* available to you, including 401(k)s and IRAs. There are others, and when you feel more comfortable you can search DailyWorth to learn more. The next question for us is what to put in those accounts. Remember, 401(k)s and IRAs are just the baskets in which your investments go. Now we have to fill up the baskets. So, what to buy? How much can you afford to invest? How will you know if your investments are performing? All good questions; all will keep you engaged.

I personally believe that the smartest way to maximize long-term gains while minimizing risk and fees is to invest in a diversified portfolio (collection) of funds. Here's the premise. All investments carry risk. Yes, risk can lose you money, but it's also what makes you money. The trick is to fill your 401(k) or IRA with a range of investments that have different levels of risk associated with them. A bond's value, for example, won't fluctuate like an EKG chart, nor will cash products like CDs (certificates of deposit). Yes, stocks can be risky. But you *absolutely must have stocks*. Stocks are where you make money. Having this variety of investments (called a *spread*) in your portfolio stabilizes the volatility of the stocks you've invested in.

Your spread protects you from the downside of risk, while allowing you to benefit from the upside. For passive investors like me (and maybe you, too), having a diversified portfolio that is allocated appropriately for your age, your risk tolerance, and your investment goals is the way to go. In general, the older you get, and the closer to retirement, the less risks you want to take. Allocating your assets according to your age, risk tolerance, and investment goals is the key to successful investing. This also means you can't just "set it and forget it." You will need to rebalance your investments as you get older, as your goals change, and if your relationship to risk shifts (if it does), or invest via a technology known as a robo-advisor that does it for you. Here are some examples of diversified portfolios, with assets allocated for age, goals, and appropriate levels of risk:

Age 25	10 percent bonds	90 percent stocks
Age 35	10 percent bonds	90 percent stocks
Age 45	20 percent bonds	80 percent stocks
Age 55	40 percent bonds	60 percent stocks

Also, make sure you look for these features in any fund you choose:

- **Solid track record:** At least a five-year history with performance in at least the top 50 percent of its category and manager tenure of at least three to five years.

- **Four or five star Morningstar rating:** High Morningstar ratings are awarded to funds that have an impressive performance history with reasonable risk and cost. "Medalist" funds—those that receive gold, silver, and bronze analyst ratings—are likely to outperform their category peers and benchmarks on a risk-adjusted basis over market cycles of at least five years. See www.morningstar.com.
- **"No-Load"** means free of sales charges.

What You Can Actually Save

Let's face it: the amount you *need* to save and invest every month might be more than what you can *actually* save and invest right now. Got big credit card debt? Got an emergency fund—one month's worth of living expenses put aside? If you're a freelancer or entrepreneur, are you saving regularly for taxes? Because you are going to be pulled in all directions when you first start thinking about what to do and how to do it, I'll give you my three rules of thumb:

1. Have at least one month's worth of living expenses saved in your emergency fund so you have cash on hand. Ideally work toward three months.
2. Pay off your expensive credit card debt first, or at least pay it way, way down. And stop getting into more debt (use your emergency fund to avoid more debt).
3. If your employer offers matching funds on your 401(k) plan, make sure you are contributing enough to get the maximum match.

If you don't have any of these things, begin by setting up the accounts. Like an empty coffee mug awaiting the morning pour. But focus on your debt first. If you're aiming for 5 percent returns on your investments while also paying 15 percent fees on your credit cards, you're not helping your net worth. Check the math. Even if your $10,000 investment earns 5 percent ($500) as you're paying 15 percent on $10,000 worth of debt ($1,500), the cost of that debt is three times your investment gains. Don't do that. You won't get out of debt quickly and you won't build your 401(k), IRA, or other accounts efficiently. You'll be working against yourself.

So have that emergency fund stocked. And when you dip into it—that's what it's for, after all—be sure to build it back up.

Emergency fund first. Debt second. Retirement third. Investments fourth.

Ridiculously Easy Cash Cows

Now, you might be thinking, okay, Amanda, I'm down with investing my money. I know why and how. But I'm just so—fill in the blank: busy/overwhelmed/risk averse/in the dark—that I'm going to hire a financial advisor in here to make sure it's done right. Stop right there. Women who face their fears of investing do much, much better than those who don't. Makes sense, right? For some, it can help to have a financial advisor. But the most important thing to do when you hire an advisor is to understand how she's managing *your* money. Otherwise—*money coma*!

"I have a wealth advisor," a major nonprofit executive told me. "I just don't know what it all means." We'll call her "Anne,"

and she is a killer fund-raiser: pitching high-net-worth investors, raising millions of dollars, and launching huge programs.
You'd think that someone like Anne would be confident with her
own investments. You would be wrong. "I'm passionate about
social enterprise," she said. "But when my [investment services]
statement comes every month, I throw it out."

She throws it out. Doesn't that sound kind of nuts? It means
she can't understand her financial advisor or double-check his
advice. She can't have a conversation with the brokerage firm
that is taking care of her money while she's busy working on
other people's bottom lines. But her aversion is common. In fact,
it's the norm.

Many women just hand off their finances and then go back
into their money stories or money comas. And here's the dirty
secret. As much as financial services want to reach women—of
course they want our money!—they know that women generally
do not know how to direct their investments and do not like the
process. Unscrupulous advisors can charge enormous fees and
ignore the portfolios—because they know women aren't going
to *ask* about them, or push them to invest better or more actively.
They make their female clients into ridiculously easy cash cows.
Don't be one of them.

It doesn't help that investment services and information historically have been poorly marketed and delivered to women.
While this blasé attitude toward female investors is shifting,
old habits die hard. So here's the deal: if you're not confident
working on your own, it's fine to work with a financial advisor. A good advisor can help you budget, plan for the financial
long-term. She can talk to you about other financial issues such
as what insurance you need, and how to make a will or a trust.

Although she will charge you a fee of 1 percent or more of your total assets, she also might end up having an even greater impact on your net worth in the long run. Now you know how to assess her value to your bottom line.

Strip Down and Be Naked

But—danger! When you work with any financial advisor, don't blindly trust them. Your financial advisor *works for you*. Know what you're invested in, know what the market is doing, generally, and know for certain that your advisor is properly accredited and working *for you*, not for commissions you know nothing about.

There are a zillion financial professionals out there with different credentials, different areas of expertise, ranges of experience, cost structures, investment minimums, money management styles, and personalities. The key to finding a good one is to ask for referrals and then shop around. Interview at least three candidates and know exactly what you're paying for. Ultimately, pick someone you trust and like. Remember, working with a financial professional can be like going to the doctor. You will need to strip down and be naked financially, and sometimes emotionally—so be prepared for that. It may be hard and it will cost you, but the objective and personalized guidance and, hopefully, peace of mind, can be well worth it.

So go in with your eyes open. Look for fiduciary advisors. Fiduciaries are legally obligated to choose investments that are in your best interests.

Here are some questions and tips to consider when you're interviewing financial advisors.

1. *How do you get paid?* Fee-only fiduciaries do not work on commissions. They typically charge a flat fee. Some charge you based on a percentage of your portfolio. For example, if you have $100,000 invested, you pay them 1 percent, or $1,000.

2. *Do you get incentives to recommend certain financial products?* Commission-based advisors get bonuses based on product sales. While the products they're selling you may be quality services and work in your best interest, your advisor is still biased.

3. *What financial services will you help me with?* You want more than just asset allocation advice. You want help with budgeting, credit, insurance, wills, and even trusts.

4. *How will you help me implement my financial plans?* Make sure you can call your advisor when you need to, and that they'll call you back.

5. *How many clients do you have like me?* You want someone who understands your level of investing, can talk straight with you, helps you to clearly understand your options, and is available for regular updates on your financial picture.

Robo-advisors

Here's a catch: many financial advisors can't afford to work with anyone with less than $500,000 in assets. Think about it. If the typical fee is 1 percent, and you have $100,000 and pay them $1,000 a year, and require a lot of their time, it doesn't compensate them relative to the time required. If you don't want to spend $3,000+ for a fee-only financial planner, you have options. Consider a robo-advisor.

Robo-adviors such as Betterment and WealthFront are wealth management systems whose advice is based on algorithms. Most robo-advisors build and rebalance your portfolio automatically. They typically charge one-quarter to one-half of what financial advisors charge. Now Vanguard, Fidelity, and Schwab offer robo-advisory services as well.

Want to learn more on your own? Financial planner Manisha Thakor recommends starting with *Little Book of Common Sense Investing* by Vanguard founder John Bogle. You could also check out *The Intelligent Investor* by Benjamin Graham. And, of course, Martin Sosnoff's *Master Class for Investors*.

An Active Passive Investor

At the end of the day (or, dare I say, the end of your life), the amount you're investing and how regularly you're investing are the most important factors. But you also need to be an active passive investor. First, don't just trust the index funds you've invested in—know the companies that make up those funds. Take one minute to do this with me. Go to Morningstar.com and search "VEA" for the Vanguard Developed Markets ETF, as an example. You will see that it is made up of individual holdings like Toyota, Nestle, and Bayer. Now you know. And tell the truth—it wasn't that hard, right? Now do this for each of the funds you're currently invested in. You're a better-informed investor with more control over your financial future when you know what you're doing.

Second, weigh the benefits and disadvantages of being socially responsible. It's one of the most frequently asked questions on DailyWorth: *How can I invest responsibly?* It's a great question and one I think about a lot. When you look at the companies that make up your mutual funds, index funds, or exchange-traded funds, you may not be happy to see companies like Monsanto (MON) or Philip Morris International (PM) listed as holdings. Sometimes socially responsible investments return less than their purely market-driven counterparts. So, to make money on your money, you may be invested in some businesses that are hurting the Earth and our human population.

Like you, I care deeply about sustainability and human rights. But we have to balance that in how we care for ourselves as well. One strategy is to include some socially screened exchange-traded funds (KLD is one) in your portfolio alongside the ones with less ideal practices that drive real profits (and better market returns).

Third, when the going gets bumpy, remember: ride it out. The sun goes up. The sun goes down. The stock market goes up. The stock market goes down. Losses are as common as gains. The only way to make money is to take on risk—it's a matter of how much risk you think you can stomach. It's inevitable that your portfolio will lose and gain money, sometimes dramatically, relative to what's happening in the overall global stock market. When you're not used to witnessing these fluctuations, it will make you queasy. But you will adjust. Get used to a new normal. Ride it out.

Finally, stay awake and keep calm before you hit the buy button. Investing is not a hard-and-fast science. It goes through trends. From IPOs to annuities to tech stocks, hot new investments dominate the news from time to time. They can entice you to make rash decisions. As with all hype, proceed with caution. Once the media is talking about it, demand will increase along with price. Don't follow the noise. Same thing goes for any investment. Including real estate: next up!

CHAPTER 7

Value Property.

Is buying a home the right investment for you?

When I bought my house in my midtwenties, I believed that all real grown-ups bought homes. It's just what you did. Unless you lived on Tornado Alley or the Jersey Shore, homes didn't disintegrate. They appreciated. Real estate, in general, was a solid investment. Or so I thought. Back then my son was just a baby, and my husband and I lived in Manhattan. We looked at what was affordable in Brooklyn: a two-bedroom apartment, far from Manhattan, with no outdoor space. For $300,000 *less*, we could get a whole lot more in Philadelphia: a huge amount of space, a real yard, *and* guest rooms in a really nice neighborhood. We could have fieldstone exterior walls, not stucco, and the understated elegance I loved. If I was going to give up New York, I thought, I might as well live it up in Philly. I just couldn't believe how much cheaper it was.

I also believed it was impossible to go wrong. We were getting such a deal by moving out of New York, and I wholeheartedly believed that homes automatically make great investments. I was in a kind of hypnosis that many people are in. I thought I knew what to do, but it turned out I didn't know anything. I was living in my fairy-tale money story, what I thought an ideal life looks like, but my ideal was all about lifestyle (appearances) and not at all about value. It turns out a lot of things we do are an extension of our stories—who we think we are, how we present ourselves, build our security, take on responsibility, handle our money (according to our MoneyType [www.moneytype.me] and our money stories—see chapter two). Often, we are driven much more by the emotional factors behind buying a home than the financial realities.

Take it from me—I bought a big house and have launched some obscenely ambitious businesses. My ambition has sunk me into some pretty deep holes. Learn from my mistakes. I now envy people who buy small. Before we met, my boyfriend bought a $250K house in a middle-lower-class neighborhood, on a rough side of the street. It was the cheaper house on the block, and it appreciated after the recession. It was a supersmart choice—solidly rooted—whereas the minimansion I bought with my ex-husband was the most expensive house on the block, whose value depreciated. Start small and live below your means until you've got a grip on what you're doing.

Welcome Home

As a kid in the late eighties, I used to watch the movie *The Money Pit*. Walter (Tom Hanks) and Anna (Shelley Long) buy a crumbling mansion for a song. It is a gorgeous renovation opportunity, they think, and they're charmed by the home's "eccentricities." But as soon as they buy it, things start to go horribly wrong. Staircases fall down. Pipes break. The front door falls out of its frame, the electrical wiring catches fire, wildlife nests in the walls—and the only contractors willing to work on the place are scam artists. The movie is a comedy, but plenty of people live some version of this home-buying hell. Though I watched this movie at least twenty times as a kid, I definitely did *not* absorb the lessons as an adult: don't get sucked into romantic ideas of real estate, specifically "home."

Where we come from shapes our identities. Where we return to night after night calms our anxieties. So it makes sense that our dwelling seems to represent our very essence. And when we *purchase* that dwelling—whether it's a house, apartment, cottage, RV, or McMansion—the emotional stakes go up exponentially. If you're single, buying your first apartment affirms your independence. If you're married, it seems to promise peace and security. In other words, it has a ton of expectations weighing on it. This idealism is especially true for people who have never owned real estate before. That's when the fantasies are strongest. We dream of who we will be when we own a home. What it will feel like to have our own piece of turf that we can fix up as we wish. White picket fence? Vegetable garden? Sandbox for the kids? Dinner parties and dinnerware? Then there's what it will mean to the world. Owning our home signals that we are grown-up, stable, committed, rooted, tasteful, productive, and valuable. We belong.

According to my friend, journalist Susan Gregory Thomas, this is especially true for Generation X. Susie wrote this back in 2009—smack in the middle of the housing crisis—and it still makes sense now.

As I sat in on marketing seminars hosted in Orlando and Anaheim, I found out that the dirt on us is that the effects of our parents' collective mass divorces of the 1970s and 1980s are clearly traceable in our behavior as parents now. We may still see ourselves as outsiders, snickering cynics who see through Baby Boomers' pretenses. But that's a big cover-up to hide that we're big mush-balls underneath. We are completely, utterly attached to our children. Generation Xers, the parents of the majority of young children now, are by all accounts the most devoted to family in American history. And we'll do whatever we have to do to keep them from having the crappy childhood that we had. . . .

In a Psychology 101 way, it kind of makes sense. One of the notorious legacies of Generation X's home-alone childhood is an abiding suspicion of authority. All this has been well documented—e.g., we hate ass-kissing the boss, so just let us do our thing because we rock as self-starters. But [t]hen the whole house bubble started to swell, and the dynamic shifted: enter the banks, as approving parents.

They gave us a home! It's almost as if we became giddy children, finally getting the apology and consolation prize we'd always secretly hoped for: you didn't get a real home as a kid, but you worked hard, succeeded on your own steam, and now we're going to give it to you and your children. . . . Welcome home. You earned it.

Except, as Susie points out—and as anyone will invariably find out—if you go into buying real estate *only* with these romantic ideas, without doing the necessary research, or having the necessary financial backup, you are in for some potentially expensive shocks.

An Emotional Decision

We've been sold on the idea that owning our own home is a sure way to build financial security and net worth. Traditional wisdom says by renting you're throwing away money every month. Buying means you're investing in a tangible asset that's going to appreciate eventually. Your money will actually go toward something you own instead of straight into your landlady's hands. But like so many other things we're talking about in this book, I have to ask: where did this idea come from? Does it always make sense to own? Does it make sense for *you* right now?

In 2012, DailyWorth's creative director, Martina Fugazzotto, bought her first apartment. Her boyfriend wasn't ready to buy, but she was. So with advice and backing from her father, Martina bought a condo of her own in a Brooklyn neighborhood that was quickly appreciating. She was about to turn thirty. It was an emotional decision. "When I was in rental spaces, I hesitated to even put up curtains because I knew I'd be leaving soon," says Martina, who had lived in five different rentals for nine years before buying. "And that just made me feel like I had no personal 'me' space."

She got her space, as well as some surprises. Four months after her purchase, the water heater exploded. At first, Martina wondered who would fix it. Then the reality sank in: it was all on *her*. She had to fix it—or hire someone herself. Welcome to home ownership.

"I was naive about this part. I didn't think there would be so many things I'd *have* to do so quickly. I had cosmetic things in mind, like one day I'd renovate the bathroom or update the kitchen." Martina, like many, had been seduced by the optics in her newly built condo. Everything was shiny and modern. But beneath the pretty looks were cheap parts and materials. "It was all built to look pretty for the sale and then just fall apart. After barely seven years, the pipes under my kitchen sink are rusted through."

Real estate is expensive up front. Sometimes it pays off. It can transform into an investment or even an income generator—a root. Martina's neighbor, who has the exact same condo, bought it for $300,000 and sold a few years later for $1 million (but note that in New York property almost always appreciates). It paid off. In spite of the headaches and repairs, Martina's purchase is likely to become a true asset, too, one day, as long as the market continues to be favorable.

People Who *Would* Make Money

But the downside can also be stark. During the 2008–2009 housing market crash, many people had put almost 0 percent down and were locked into ridiculous mortgage terms. (The National Association of Realtors reported that in 2005 and 2006 four out of ten—an incredibly high number—of first-time buyers had put *nothing* down at all, and many had put just 2 percent down.) They watched as their home values plummeted well below the equity they had tied up in them. In other words, they had almost nothing invested in their homes, yet they were liable for paying off their inflated loans. That meant sudden and massive debt, the kind some people could never pay off. The bubble created extraordinary circumstances, for sure, but if buyers had a tiny bit of knowledge, they might have understood that they were signing up for huge problems. They could have avoided disaster. But many of us didn't.

Again, Susie's take still makes sense:

Generation X [was] much more likely to look at their home as an investment than previous generations, owing largely—you guessed it—to having lived through the '90s recession, followed by the stock market losses in the early '00s. For those of us crawling our way out of the wreckage of the dot-bomb period, that's what made those low- or no-down-payment and ARM mortgages so irresistible. Indeed, surveys conducted by the National Association of Realtors show that four out of ten first-time buyers used no-money-down mortgages in 2005 and 2006; the median down payment for first-time buyers in those years was just two percent.

What this seems to mean is that the collective feeling was, basically: screw stocks, invest in a home, pay for it when you get back on your feet. This seemed like a no-brainer for phoenix-like Gen Xers. After all, in spite of the pronouncement of a much-cited 2004 study of generational differences, Gen X "went through its all-important, formative years as one of the least parented, least nurtured generations in US history." Half of all Gen X children's families split, and forty percent were latchkey kids—we'd always not only landed on our feet but kicked some serious booty, too.

[A Harvard report confirmed] "that Gen Xers have more actual or perceived opportunities for upward financial mobility." Far be it from the banks to have disabused anyone of that notion. Personal anecdote: after signing onto a five-year ARM mortgage in 2002, I remember the loan officer at WaMu telling my husband and me that although we were cash poor now, he could tell that we were the kind of people who *would* make money in the future. We were the kind of people, he said, that the bank wanted to "invest in."

That false confidence led to many, many Faustian deals. It did for Susie, for me, and for the economy as a whole. Don't let it happen to you.

A Tree Falls

Think of it this way. You are sinking hundreds of thousands of dollars into something that will be mostly owned by the mortgage lender for a very long time. It's not a root until *you* (not the bank) own a substantial part of it—for example, if you make a significant down payment or pay off a lot of the mortgage. The worth of your home grows slowly, often more slowly than retirement savings accounts. And, unlike stocks, real estate has surprise expenses—a tree falls on your roof, the boiler blows, the windows crack or leak. You need the ongoing financial means to repair these. How fluffy is your cushion?

For many people, a home is a "buy and hold" investment (except for those who flip houses or are extremely wealthy). The value of a home is subject to the fluctuations of the market. It also requires a lot of hands-on attention. Both of these factors can eat into your long-term picture by tying up your cash flow for years. "I have a spreadsheet that lists everything I need to fix in my home in order of urgency," says Martina, today a reformed real estate romantic. "I'm just going down the list each month. For Christmas, my dad even contributed to the 'fix the bathroom' fund!" Happy holidays.

Just Buy Anything

Let's take a closer look at what makes investing in real estate a great root—and when to make a different choice. Gina DeVee, a successful coach and creator of *Divine Living*, a luxury magazine for women entrepreneurs, says that, like many women, she wasn't in a position to buy a house at the beginning of her career. When she started making good money, the pressure to buy property ramped up. *Just buy anything* was the message. Snap it up and stop throwing your money away. Who cares if you're living in a dump or in a part of town no one has heard of. Invest in real estate.

But being an entrepreneur, she approached it in a different way. "Before making any moves, I looked more closely at the costs of buying, and suddenly this rule stopped making sense to me [when] I started to add up how much money I'd need for a down payment, what I would owe in taxes, plus the maintenance costs, renovations, not to mention what I'd spend on furnishing the house," she says. "I realized I was not going to get to live in a place I actually wanted to live in, and it'd be really expensive for where I was at financially—plus did I really want to be focusing on a house while I was growing my business?"

This approach served her well. She decided that instead of buying, she would upgrade her lifestyle, allowing her to entertain high-end clients and throw exclusive parties in her luxury rental. She stopped her lease whenever she traveled extensively, and weathered the real estate market crash in 2008 without any loss. Good research, listening to her gut, and making unemotional decisions helped Gina to do what she really needed for *her* life. That is the whole point.

The Joint Center for Housing Studies at Harvard University's 2016 report found that nearly 40 percent of Americans are renting—an all-time high since the mid-1960s. Is it better for your financial health to rent or own right now? You can find out by looking at a rent-versus-buy calculator (Google it) online. The *New York Times*, Bankrate, and Schwab all have them. There's nothing like seeing the numbers to make your decision come to life. If you decide to rent, consider putting the money you would have used for a mortgage/maintenance costs into your 401(k) or IRA instead. Mortgages can be considered enforced savings plans; if you're a renter, why not up the stakes on yourself? That's a very good investment.

Who Doesn't Want a Deal?

Let's look at some more facts and situations that make your purchase of a home worth it in dollars, as well as in feelings. It comes down to who you are and where you are in your life. How much do you make? Will you make more? When? How much debt are you in? What's your credit score? How much do you have saved? There are no hard-and-fast rules, only guiding principles and the resilience to stay awake during the learning process. If you've never owned before, it's a good idea to start small. Buy a starter house. It's a lot harder to work backward from a minimansion, which is what I did. In fact, after owning—and getting into plenty of hot water—I now rent. It's true. Renting makes more sense for me right now.

Also, have a good grasp on what you can afford and what kinds of loans are available. Banks may approve you for mortgages that are much higher than what your own calculations show you can afford. Just because the bank (or other lender) says it doesn't make it true. Who doesn't want a deal? If you can get away with putting less down for your house, why wouldn't you do that? Because, as financial advisor Carmen Rita Wong says, you need to have skin in the game. How much you put down affects what interest rate you get on your mortgage. Very little down (say, 3–5 percent of the home's selling price) means your mortgage will have a higher interest rate because *you* are considered higher risk. And you won't be able to borrow against your house for some time—because, effectively, it's not really yours. Someone else (the bank, the government) owns most of your house. You will be paying interest for a lot longer, meaning that it will take even longer for your monthly payment to purchase actual equity in your home. There's no root in that!

Coming up with a healthy 20 percent down payment can seem daunting. Maybe you need a smaller house? A condo, even? If you want to be able to meet this challenge, you're going to have a lot more to deal with as a home owner, so it's best to know if you're cash-flow ready from the outset. Plus, if you put a healthy amount down, you'll own more equity if you do need to sell it. "You can much more easily sell a losing stock at a loss than sell a house that you not only have lost money in but that you don't have a dime invested in," says Rita Wong.

Paying for a Loan

Resist temptation. Stick to your numbers. A mortgage, after all, is a loan to buy a home. Your home is the collateral for that loan. When you apply for a mortgage, will you get a fifteen-year or thirty-year term? Thirty-year mortgages mean you pay less month by month, but at a higher interest rate, so you'll pay more interest longer and gain equity more slowly over time.

For example, over the life of a $100,000, thirty-year mortgage at 5 percent, you'll pay 360 monthly payments of $477 each, totaling $171,870. That means you're paying $71,870 in interest to borrow $100,000. And remember that initially most or all of your payments will be interest, not principal (equity), so you're *paying* for a *loan* to maintain the *home equity* you bought from your *down payment*. Over the first ten years, the only appreciation you stand to gain on your home? Market appreciation. With a fifteen-year mortgage, you're at an advantage because you'll pay less in interest and gain home equity faster—which directly factors into your net worth. That's what we want.

No matter what, when you buy a home, either be sure it will appreciate in value or that you plan to stay there for at least ten years. Otherwise, your home purchase is a *lifestyle* choice, not a contributor to your personal net worth. And be smart about the mortgage you get. It's shocking, but many people don't shop around for a mortgage. The Consumer Financial Protection Bureau found that nearly half of home buyers do not look for mortgages with more favorable interest rates. Why?

They're intimidated by the process. Don't give in to your

money stories or fall into a money coma. Once you get past the jargon, it's not complicated. Learn how the game is played and get the best rates you can. Remember—your money, *your terms*. Stay in the game and get the best rates going. When thinking about what you can afford, you want to weigh your long-term financial health against your immediate happiness and come up with a balanced solution.

Homes Are Hungry

Buying a house incurs a lot of up-front costs. For the first few years, you're only paying interest on the mortgage. Then there're all the costs of getting into the house—the lawyer, inspectors, tests (for asbestos, lead, and radon), moving, new furniture, immediate repairs, plus any surprises. If for some reason you need to sell in a few years, you'll either lose money or break even, unless you're in a really, really hot neighborhood.

It happens—people relocate for jobs, go through breakups and need to split, or have family emergencies that pull them elsewhere. Housing prices also fluctuate with the economy. This means if you buy now and sell quickly you could end up selling for less than what you paid. Ouch. Expensive. It's best—if you can—to live in your home for a minimum of five years. Or, better yet, ten years. Or more. If you know you're going to stick around and you know that your income is going to grow or at least stay stable, by all means consider buying.

Plus, homes are hungry. Homes eat money. Once you've bought your house, the day-to-day expenses start. Your utility bills could be three times what you paid when you rented.

And there are property taxes—charges for water, garbage collection, etc. And the yard? Who's going to prune the shrubs and weed the flower beds? The best way to ensure that you can meet these costs—and still have anything close to a life—is to make sure that you *make enough money*. "Never pay more than a year's worth of your gross household income in mortgage debt. This rule will force you to take the emotion out of the purchase and perceive a house as four walls and a roof, with a liability wrapped around it," notes Richard Rosso, a certified financial planner from Houston, Texas.

What's your monthly salary? Have enough inflow of cash, otherwise you'll be "house poor"—trapped, financially, by your house. That's horrible. Before you commit to buying, make sure that you can afford to spend 30 percent (no more) of your pretax income every month on house-related costs. That includes your mortgage payments, property taxes, utilities, repairs, and renovations. Here's a challenge for you: don't buy a house until you have half of the home purchase price in liquid cash. So, if you're buying a $300,000 home, have $150,000 saved. Think I'm crazy? Ask someone who has lived in a house for five-plus years to add up all they've spent on their home. It will be closer to half of the home value than you realize. Not even the shrewdest home inspector can warn you about every eventuality, so you're going to need to provide your own backup. You won't be able to save or invest outside of your house. Why stretch yourself so painfully? Look for a situation that won't bankrupt your life.

You should also be pretty certain that your income will keep increasing—or at least keep pace with inflation (3 percent). Everything gets more expensive over time, and property values can go up unexpectedly. Just ask residents of Chicago, whose property taxes will increase 13 percent between 2016 and 2019.

Transformed into a Root

When you've recovered financially from the initial hefty outlay of purchasing a home (which could take several years), you may start to see the benefits of home ownership. As you pay down your mortgage and its interest, you have increasing equity. Your purchase becomes an asset that you could potentially borrow against. Your net worth increases. If you really need to, you could sell. If you don't sell, and you stay put until the end of your mortgage, you will own the property outright, giving you physical security for the rest of your life and freeing up your money as you get older. Your expensive purchase has transformed into a root. Congratulations.

I want to tell you an incredible success story, because up until now in this chapter, I've just been issuing warnings about how home ownership does not necessarily guarantee security. But it is possible to do well with real estate. Even though its value typically grows more slowly than 401(k)s or IRAs (or other market-based investments), property can produce liquidity (access to cash) or income in the way that investments can't. Hooray! That can be significant.

In October 2012, Kelsey Dixon and her new husband bought their first home, a two-unit residential building in York, Pennsylvania, where they are from. They had just graduated from college, had landed jobs in their fields, and had a combined savings of $35,000. Impressive, right? In fact, she had plans to be net worth positive as far back as high school (eye roll—I know!).

"I'm a believer that savings, money, and investments should be working for you and never just sitting stale," she says confidently. Her family and husband supported that. She was also fortunate that her hometown was fairly small and affordable, meaning they could buy.

In their new home, Kelsey and Wes lived in one half of the building and rented the other half. They had to make some immediate improvements that ran them an extra $10,000 off the bat: the furnace needed to be replaced, and they added a dishwasher and central air-conditioning. They renovated the top floor to include a bedroom and full bathroom. But then the renovations allowed Kelsey to increase the rent on the second unit by 25 percent. Their monthly mortgage was just over $1,000, and their tenant paid $650. Smart.

One year later, Kelsey and Wes took the rest of their savings and bought an investment property. Wow. "Wes is a handyman," says Kelsey. "I'm a people person. Buying investment properties and being landlords suited us. We rented to people twice our age." It also helped that Kelsey's brother-in-law and father-in-law are in electricity and construction, so they pitched in to help renovate the second property. The place also needed a new roof, new driveway, and new appliances, so they spent all their savings plus borrowed money to fix the place up. Then they got renters in. "We were quickly able to get back on our feet. We filled the units for $600 and $650 a month. Our mortgage was only $463 a month." Sweet.

But by the middle of 2014, at the tender age of twenty-four, Kelsey and her husband had owned property for two years. Being young, they were getting restless. Wes wanted to try something different from his white-collar job, and the couple wasn't ready to have kids. "We wanted to explore the world and try new things with our careers," says Kelsey, now twenty-five. "So we gave up our great jobs, packed our car, and landed in Seattle, Washington—to explore."

Wes's brother was left in charge of property details as needed. Kelsey started her own marketing firm for companies that want to reach millennials, and Wes got work as a carpenter apprentice. "We make twelve thousand dollars a year from our properties, which almost pays for our rent in Seattle. We should be able to pay off our second home within the next ten years. That means when we're thirty-five years old, we'll be making one hundred percent of our income from the two units, not including pop-up expenses, of course," she says. Kelsey feels lucky and grateful to have had such a strong start. "Creating roots early on helped us accomplish our goals and get after our dreams. This is only the beginning!" She and Wes have dreams to volunteer in Chile and learn Spanish, backpack in Asia, and work in Europe, and eventually go back to Pennsylvania and start a family. The possibilities, she says, are endless. Talk about playing your cards right. Sheesh.

Working to Her Advantage

What can you learn from Kelsey? I don't want to mislead you: part of her success *was* luck. She was from a town that had affordable property. She had family who could help her out with renovations, wiring, and plumbing, which saved her a lot of money and headaches. She had a lucrative job during college that allowed her to save significantly. Not everyone is going to have such a head start. But her story has plenty to teach, too. A big reason she succeeded is that she had the mind-set of a saver and investor.

Kelsey valued staying out of debt and building savings. And she didn't simply hang on to her money. She *invested* it. She saw a good opportunity, partnered up with her husband and her family, and took a calculated risk. She bought property, renovated it, and rented it out. In her early twenties, she knew nothing about being a landlady. But she learned. Kelsey was strategic. She didn't get cash poor in the process of buying real estate. She *could* have bought a money pit, but she didn't. She made a considered choice. She *could* have been overwhelmed by property management or the rental market. But she educated herself about pricing, collecting rent, utilities, insurance, fees, and so on. Because she was methodical, she worked her way through all the unknowns and made her circumstances—and her resources—work to her advantage.

The ideal is to build roots and wings at the same time. Kelsey figured out how to have both: First, a robust savings account allowed her to invest in roots. Then the roots actually started to support her wings by producing income she could live on. Most of us wait until we're older to see such great payoffs. Well done, Kelsey—even if we're just a little bit jealous.

Blast the Heat

Resist the temptation to stretch beyond your means. There are all kinds of temptations to live large right away. But you don't want to back yourself into a financial corner, especially when you're starting out. Buy in a city, neighborhood, and block that are coming up but haven't peaked. Kelsey and her husband bought in a small town where a two-unit place cost them $140,000. That's affordable, much more so than, say, New York City or San Francisco. (Note that I'm *not* telling you to move. But if you can, and it will mean you can get in the game, it might make sense. Up to you.)

Look at the houses on your ideal block—how much did they sell for? How much are they currently worth? Don't buy the most expensive one. Buy one whose value—as far as you can estimate—will likely appreciate. Know if you are DIY inclined. Yes? Then you could consider a fixer-upper. Not so much? Think about how much extra you'll have to take out to renovate—and how much of your life you can afford to spend managing the renovation. Do it if you have the patience and budget to handle *twice* what you project renovations will cost. It always takes longer, costs more, and uncovers issues you didn't know previously existed. Know as much as you can about yourself and the context you're getting into. It's all useful information.

Rushing to make an offer, to close, skipping the inspection and final walk-through, not researching house values in your neighborhood—and on your block—going with the first mortgage offer, or broker—all of these are expensive mistakes. Don't rush. Give yourself several months to look at neighborhoods, interview agents, and consider loans and money-saving programs. Maybe plan to rent in the neighborhood for a year until you're really sure you know which block you want to live on. Give yourself time to investigate.

If you've been renting for a while, you might assume, like Cynthia Ramnarace did, that home shopping is similar to hunting for a rental: you might go in wondering if there are enough closets and outlets or if you like the view. Turns out, these are not the things to look at. You want to get superpractical. Open doors, lift up carpets, bring a flashlight, ask lots and lots of questions. Cynthia and her husband learned to be pragmatists the hard way. "Buying a home is more like buying a used car than renting an apartment. You need to look under the hood and take it for a spin. Turn on all the faucets. Flush the toilet. Blast the heat and see what happens."

The average home search takes twelve weeks, according to the National Association of Realtors. Closing takes another three to four months, on average. And before the shopping or closing even happen, you have to do your own research and reflecting, too. I'd say take anywhere from two to twelve months. The slow and steady approach is worth it. It can save you tens of thousands of dollars over time. And it gives you time to face your fantasies and fears head-on, and come back down to earth, down to what you can afford without having a heart attack each month when your mortgage is due, or when you have a mouse infestation, or your little cousin brings bedbugs back from Bali.

Make sure there's a market for the property you're buying. Meaning, if you wanted to sell it, would you find a buyer? Would you get more than you paid for it? There was a time when, at twenty-five, I considered buying a houseboat on the edge of Manhattan. It was a five-star, ninety-five-foot, stylishly renovated tugboat. I was looking at the boat like an apartment. Then someone pulled me aside. "Amanda, only someone like you would ever want to buy it." Meaning there was not a market for this kind of property. In fact, there was zero evidence that I would even make back my initial investment. I'd likely lose hundreds of thousands of dollars if I ever wanted to sell. There's just not much demand for a houseboat on the Hudson.

So, unless you can afford to lose big-time, consider the potential resale value of your real estate. Just because you'll pay for something doesn't mean anyone else will. Buy smart—and renovate intelligently, too. Don't coast on the idea that "I'll make it back." You might not.

Chief Problem Solver

Let's quickly address flipping, or buying real estate, and fixing it up with the idea of selling it off quickly at a profit. While it sounds lucrative and looks fun on HGTV, flipping is only for those who can stomach the risky ride. You need a significant amount of cash on hand for the initial output (down payment, closing costs, materials, labor). You need to become the chief problem solver who can tackle all the unforeseen issues—practical, financial, and interpersonal. They are guaranteed to come up. And, typically, projects go way over budget and over time. Can you handle that? There can definitely be a thrill in taking a property from unremarkable to noteworthy and profitable. It's a lot of hard work, but the upside can be big. It's also high risk. You also have to be okay if you don't make your money back. Because there's always a chance you'll be stuck with something you never wanted in the first place.

Many of us are eager to own our own homes. It has a powerful emotional resonance. But if you can make buying a house or an apartment less of an emotional or lifestyle investment (*I'm a grown-up now; I own a home! I've made it*) and more about your long-term financial health, your head is going to be clearer around the hundreds of thousands of dollars you're about to spend. That clear-eyed approach is what helped Kelsey and her husband make good choices. You can, too.

CHAPTER 8

Run the Show.

Launch a business for fun and profit—if you're cut out for it.

Businesses can make phenomenal roots. In fact, they are the most effective route to creating unlimited wealth, teaching you about how money works, and controlling your own destiny—big-time. I can tell you from personal experience that it is a thrill to establish and run a business. I have done it several times across retail, technology, media, and now finance. And even the businesses that were technically failures have taught me an enormous amount—like how to run a profit and loss statement, read a balance sheet, and collect receivables—and led me to creating DailyWorth.

But as exciting as this root is, it has a huge catch. The risk can easily outweigh the effort required. The initial *years* it takes to prove your business idea, reach customers, and then grow profits and maybe seek outside capital is risky at every turn. It takes a toll on your savings, your career, your relationships, and your equanimity. Running a business can be a root, just like owning real estate and investing in the stock market. But, unless you're already a business owner, chances are you're not quite aware of the difference between running a business and being a freelancer (or being self-employed). The differences cannot be overstated.

A Powerful Reason

Our culture has a bizarre worship of self-made moguls of today, such as Richard Branson and Tim Ferriss, without much understanding of how they got there. As if freedom and money just happens once you figure out your "thing." Don't be fooled. Both owning a biz and being a freelancer require a lot of tenacity and responsibility. But one *grows your value*; the other just *covers your paycheck*. For my purposes, there's only one that is a root: a business that has value to someone other than you. Got that?

Let me break it down a different way. If you're just aiming to become self-employed or an independent contractor (alternate terms for freelancer), you won't be creating a root, an entity that one day could run without you. It's fine to be a freelancer, don't get me wrong. But it's a choice. A freelance business doesn't exist without *your* time, *your* skill, *your* sweat equity. Your brand IS you. This means that your solo work is pretty much just another job: if you go away, so does the business. When you create a *root*, however, the idea is you can hand over some—or all—of the key functions to someone else, for a price, and they can run it or even own it outright. You walk away with money in your pocket.

So know what you're getting into. Are you going to work your tail off just to earn an income? Is that really better than your job was? Or are you interested in creating something that one day could make you profits *and* run without you? Or one that you could potentially sell or get others to invest in heavily?

In my experience, you have to have a driving passion for your business. Because the day-to-day mechanics are hard. Things are going to go up, down, and sideways on any given day. You have to have the ability to weather the rejections and failure you will absolutely encounter until, or if, your business starts to make money. Even things that should go right don't. Everything takes more time than you think it should, and every three months or so there's some long vacation where everyone goes away. You still have payroll to fund even when no one is around to buy your goods. It's the "argh" factor in being an entrepreneur. This is true whether you're selling a product on the side or running a full-time services business with employees.

So, you may be asking, why risk burning out your passion by piling on the hassles? Administration (bookkeeping, invoicing, dealing with vendors), dealing with finicky customers and reluctant investors—that doesn't sound like too much fun. How do you even keep going?

You need a powerful reason. You keep going because you believe you are making a difference. You can smell potential in the air, and you can see a future that makes sense to you. You're making digital games that empower teenage girls. That gets you out of bed in the morning, and keeps you pushing through all the snags and the nos. You're bringing herbal remedies to women who want to conceive. You also like having more control over your input and output. You enjoy the challenge. You may even thrive on adrenaline.

Personally, I have a big dream of how I want the world to be different. When I started DailyWorth, people snickered. But I knew they were wrong. I'm motivated by both social impact and financial success. The chance to improve the lives of countless women is what keeps me going when producing the actual business gets stressful.

Not Going to Lie

Running a business is not out of reach for you, either. Today, more and more women are running small businesses. In 2015, nearly 30 percent of small businesses were run by women, according to the Institute for Women's Policy Research. That's an almost 70 percent increase from 2007—huge growth. The numbers of minority women running businesses are growing exponentially, too. For women who feel like there aren't enough opportunities in established careers, businesses present unlimited possibilities.

In running a business, you are aiming to do more than just survive. You're aiming to build wealth more efficiently than you could as an employee. You are aiming to fully stock your retirement accounts as well as creating a wide professional network and more opportunities for growth. Keep thinking big. I didn't stop at Soapbxx, and wasn't deterred by the two other businesses I started (and sank money into) that didn't go anywhere. I knew I had big work to do. It just took me some time to learn my audience, refine my ideas and my delivery. All of that is normal. You may aim smaller than I did (my risk tolerance is unusually high, I know), but you can also have well-diversified roots in your garden.

Running a business is about having power, influence, and creative control. And to do that, you have to be willing to take risks and ride the roller coaster of uncertainty to get there. But I'm not going to lie to you: nine out of ten businesses fail. This root is the trickiest of the bunch. But when you're an employee, you work hard for someone else, and there's no real security. Sure, the steady paycheck and benefits get comfortable, the annual cost-of-living raise is great, and so is the occasional promotion. But at any point your income could disappear.

There's company restructuring and downsizing. There are the ongoing changes in technology. For example, a 2013 study by Oxford University found that of 702 occupations—a lot—nearly 50 percent would soon be replaced by computers and machines. You could get laid off or downsized for any number of reasons (stress!), nixing the investment of your time and effort. The potential for huge financial growth as an employee is also pretty limited. Proof: the top people—at least the first two hundred—in Forbes's billionaire list are *not* employees (and, yes, several of them *are* women). They landed there through entrepreneurship, not as nine-to-fivers.

No One *Makes* You

Maybe you don't care about billionaires. You just want to be self-employed or a freelancer. I hear you. But here, I'm focusing on businesses as roots, specifically how you turn a business that you own into an asset that has significant value (by way of revenue or the potential to be bought) outside of the time you put into doing the work. When you are free to make your own profits, you set the terms. The personal satisfaction can be high. No one *makes* you do anything. It's your dream, your vision, your schedule. Yes, you will make mistakes, but you've got skin in the game, and that's exhilarating. If you long to chart your own course, want the freedom to creatively problem-solve, and the potential to make much more money than you ever could as an employee, a business is the way to go.

According to recent Gallup poll numbers, almost 70 percent of employees are disengaged from their work, and a full 50 percent want to quit. People want greater freedom to control their schedules. They want more work/life balance and the possibility of more income. If you troll around online—and who doesn't?—you may have noticed there's a lot of talk about a 1-2-3-step process to becoming a successful small business owner, whether as a solopreneur (edible garden designer?), a star blogger (The Secret Diary of a Ninja Mom?), or microbrand starter (Greek olive oil imports?). The promise is that you can build healthy profits from home on your own schedule. Be a real business breakout.

With a few exceptions—like what entrepreneurial coaches Marie Forleo, Ramit Sethi, and Tara Gentile teach—most of it is hype. Although *some* people make these businesses work exactly as scripted, there *ain't no 1-2-3 simple strategy*. It is a dream that you can just fill out some paperwork, flip a few switches, and then start making good money. In my experience, you work hard for two years before you reach a magic sweet spot where opportunities start to pop. It takes at least six months to plan any business and another two years of seed planting before real revenue sprouts. Anything new takes time to get traction. And that's *if* you're running the *right* business, one that can actually turn a profit.

Actually, a big problem is the mental game itself. You might feel like an impostor: I'm not an *entrepreneur*! Again, as we've seen over and over again throughout this book, there is great power in recognizing that you're a novice: that means you're open to learning. When you are not mired in conventional practices, you can ask questions that haven't been asked before or look at problems in ways others haven't seen.

Consider pharmaceutical behemoth Eli Lilly, for example. The company created a crowdsourcing division called InnoCentive: "outsiders" are paid to figure out problems the company can't solve. It works. Many problems are solved by those from outside the field in question, according to a study by Karim Lakhani of Harvard Business School. Feel like an impostor? You might have the most important point of view of all. As Tina Fey once quipped, "I've realized that almost everyone is a fraud, so I try not to feel too bad about it."

Hardly All Roses

You're bored. You're done with commuting, shrinking budgets, and micromanaging supervisors. You're done with missing your kid's performances. You're done with not having enough influence or enough money. You want to live like your Facebook friends and head to Mexico for an entire month in February for "personal development" retreats. Or maybe your work environment is so toxic that your mental and physical health depend on you leaving. You want to go freelance.

When you freelance, you essentially run a services business. You offer your skills and products to people who need them (for a rate that's based on your time or on the scope of the project). All the work relies on your ability to produce and deliver. You are the kingpin. This is an appealing idea to a lot of people. In 2016, fifty-three million people—34 percent of the population—were freelancing, a big jump from 2004 numbers (42.6 million). When you factor in workplace dissatisfaction, commute time, and inflexible schedules, freelancing makes sense for a lot of people.

You might become a freelancer by accident—or by circumstance. You became a mom and need the flexibility; you got laid off or downsized and don't care to go through that again; you were overlooked for a promotion and quit, looking for a better way. On the upside, you can work at home in your yoga pants and not leave the house until three p.m. You can take Wednesday off and work Sunday night instead. You can make your sister's birthday lunch, take care of your sick dog, and get through a snowstorm without an interruption. And on good months, when lots of checks come in, you feel rich.

Even as the "gig economy" is growing (40 percent of the US workforce in 2016 and expected to rise), does it really make sense to trade financial stability for flexibility so flexible that you can't afford to leave the house? (And your first couple of years may feel like that.) Freelancing is hardly all roses. You don't make money when you can't produce or deliver (you're sick, your kids are sick, you have tech issues, etc.). I never got a maternity leave with either kid. You may take a month "off," but you'll be on your laptop on that beach in Costa Rica scrambling to find reliable Wi-Fi. Trust me, it's grating.

In other words, the *free* in *freelance* can be misleading. You're going to work hard—maybe harder than ever before. Your income will be unpredictable, and in the meantime your bills for health insurance, car payments, etc., will continue to pile up. Because life doesn't stop, even when your clients pay late. As a freelancer or gig jockey, you do all the work, make all the decisions, do the billing, and cover the expenses. You hustle to get work, and then you hustle to get your clients to pay you. And, from a day-to-day finance point of view, when you leave your full-time job (or you have to leave), you essentially leave behind a steady paycheck, benefits, paid vacation, and sick leave. For what? How long will it take you to start contributing to your retirement savings again?

It *is* possible to make more money outside of a traditional office environment. In fact, your potential to create huge personal worth and have real financial security is very limited as an employee; being an employee is, technically speaking, not a good investment. It's also possible to feel so lonely, so terrified, and so broke that you'll go running right *back* to the office. Most people leap without understanding that there are different ways to do this, and choosing the right one depends on who you are and what you want. Many people leap without looking. Don't do that.

Massive Growth

To run a *business*, you need the same grit and resolve you need as a freelancer, but you also need to think beyond what you need for today or next month. If you can make it through the painful uncertainty of the first year or two of a new business, you may very well start making enough money to live on. You may be making what you did in the office—or more. But you need to go beyond income and lifestyle success to make your business a root—something that someone else can invest in or buy from you. Your hustle alone does not create a root.

To begin, you need a healthy savings account as well as the discipline to learn new skills on the fly, find resources where and when you need them, network like a pro, bill for your work, follow up on leads—all those things that don't directly make you money but that absolutely keep your business viable. You have to learn to sell yourself, sell your services, and close deals. You have to make yourself visible and your worth obvious. You have to master the "everything is awesome" smiley face.

You need to think big, big picture: What can I put my time and energy into that will create profits that far exceed my expenses? How can I automate processes or make services repeatable at a low time or energy cost to me or my staff? At my engineering company, Soapbxx, we built complex websites with video, e-commerce, and online communities. At first, I programmed our websites myself, but I quickly learned that to succeed, I needed to manage operations and sales instead. To be successful I'd have to learn the art and science of selling anything—luckily, I also discovered that I *loved* sales. I hired others (programmers, designers, etc.) to do my job.

In two years, Soapbxx had grown so much that I had five full-time employees. I worked two hours a day; my staff did the rest. That may sound like success, but it wasn't *ultimate* success. It's not just the freedom to work so little (lifestyle choice) that signals that you've "made it." Soapbxx still wasn't quite yet a root for me. It was technically successful; it was profitable, and it allowed me to retain control and equity while I barely worked at all.

But it was hard to scale, meaning we had to give every new project our full focus and attention. There was nothing we could automate or replicate or template. That's costly. Even as our revenue climbed to $1 million, so did expenses. Then there was the gargantuan tax bill that almost sank me. Soapbxx was a productivity machine, but each new project required so much planning and management that margins ran thin.

When your business is a root, there is the potential for *massive* growth (not just some growth). You can replicate services to keep costs down. And people other than you see the potential for profits to increase. Think about it: if an investor gives you backing (for example, $100,000 or more), she is gambling that your business will grow and make her money back—and then some. And first she wants to see evidence that this is possible. Who would put money behind a business that isn't showing customer adoption?

Soapbxx was a services company at its heart, but eventually it did function as a root—above and beyond creating a nice income for me. Here's how: it provided the $20,000 in seed money I needed to get DailyWorth off the ground. I was able to assign my Soapbxx engineers the task of creating and maintaining the existence of DailyWorth for two years. And because I was getting a healthy income from Soapbxx, I was able to work for DailyWorth for free for the first two years of its existence. That was important. That's how long it took me to prove that DailyWorth had the audience, traffic, and sales traction that potential investors wanted to see. I could present DailyWorth as a business worth investing money into. It had a clear path to profitability.

Essentially, Soapbxx funded DailyWorth, and once Daily-Worth was a business (had investors; could be sold), I dissolved Soapbxx. I went from working two hours a day to raising money from investors and troubleshooting big operational juggernauts. The other way I know DailyWorth is a root is that today the next step is what's called a liquidity event. That's the moment when the value of DailyWorth *on paper* is translated into cold, hard cash via an IPO, an acquisition, or a merger. Until then, I'm building a significant root, but I don't have access to its full power—yet. I have no access to that equity. But there's tremendous potential.

Sarah Kunst, a young entrepreneur (and millennial) in Silicon Valley, sees the investing choices that more established women in tech are *not* making. She watches men at the same pay grade and skill level take risks and create enormously powerful networks and businesses. "A lot of guys seem to understand that you have to spend money and take calculated risks, whereas there's just a kind of reluctance on women's part to do this," she told me. Sarah wants to be on the right side of this gap, and so do you. She's created her own business, building her networks and investing.

They Can Be Sold

Money doesn't flock to great ideas. It accumulates around a great *execution*. This is where a lot of people go wrong. Just because you have a great idea doesn't mean people are going to buy what you are selling. I've launched and folded multiple concepts that people loved in theory (so they told me) but wouldn't pay for. As many people find out the hard way, running a business is 10 percent creating and 90 percent sales and marketing. You have to reach people; your business has to provide something that people want, and they need to know about it so they can spend money on it.

No matter what size your venture—from a one-woman show

that starts in your closet, to an incorporated business with employees and overhead—you're going to need to deeply understand sales and be able to close on leads. Create pipelines—broad prospects that narrow down to viable possibilities and, finally, real customers. You need cash flow to develop your business (wings), let people know about it (advertising and marketing), entice them to buy it (sales), and keep reaching new clients (networking, audience development).

A viable business has several things that make it valuable. It has assets beyond the money it generates: a product (e.g., technology or goods to sell); revenue-generating assets (contracts); hardware (equipment, computers, desks, etc.); intellectual property; goodwill (a visible brand; a strong reputation). All these things are worth money. They can be assigned a dollar value—and they can be sold. They are separate from your personal assets or contributions.

To Build a Business

In 2008, Adda Birnir was working at a digital photography studio. She'd gone from print to digital to stay ahead in a very quickly changing industry. Then the markets crashed and all the nontechnical people were laid off, including her. Suddenly jobless, Adda decided to learn the technical side of the business: computer programming. She eventually got another full-time position, where she met a coworker and together they launched their own business. Except Adda had no idea what she was doing. "That was the first business that I created, but I just stumbled into it," she says. "We had an eight-thousand-dollar contract and one client; I ran the business for a couple of months before

I actually understood that that's what I was doing, running a business."

Today, a couple of businesses later, Adda runs Skillcrush, an online company that teaches computer programming to women. It's an underserved market, so there's lots of room for growth. Adda built Skillcrush as a brand intentionally so that she could hire junior teachers while focusing on scale. This frees up her time to grow the company's services, its reach, and its profits. Adda wasn't born into a business family, and she doesn't have an MBA. In fact, she started off her working life thinking she was going to be a photographer. But step by step, she learned to build a business that has real potential to be sold, building her wealth in the long term.

Though Adda currently makes less than she would in a corporate programming job with the same responsibilities, her long-term earning potential is ten times what she would make at a job. She employs ten people and business is pumping. She'll hopefully benefit from that in the future—either through wildly increased profits or a "liquidity event"—when someone else buys Skillcrush. Although she hasn't reached consistent profitability yet, she's getting there after five years of nonstop hustle.

Take Me to the Bridge

When your revenue exceeds your operating costs, you're paying yourself, people know about you, and your business is growing without you having to manage every single aspect of it, then you've arrived. Congratulations. Your business is now a root. Until that day, start by choosing a less risky way to test the waters. Run a side business without quitting your regular job.

Invest in an existing business. At the very least, think to yourself, *Take me to the bridge!* That is, take a bridge job to help you
make the leap between your career and your business venture.

When the call is strong to set out on your own, it's tempting
to jump right away. Your friends might say: *Follow your dreams
and you can't fail!* You can. But in my experience, rent, cell phones,
cars, and groceries are not made of dreams. They cost money.
To survive while you're making your dreams a reality—for example, while you're still learning which expenses are business
expenses and which are personal—you still have to live.

Getting your business off the ground is the not-so-glamorous
part of being your own boss. It's when you patch things together, borrow from friends, scrimp on your own lifestyle. It
rarely makes the headlines. Many successful business owners,
such as Nisha Moodley, worked two (or more) jobs until their
dream businesses started to show steady profits. As I've said, it
took two years before DailyWorth started to get any traction.
And in that time I was still running my computer programming
company, Soapbxx, with a toddler and an infant in tow.

Brand developer Kristen Domingue tells her cautionary tale
about how she left her full-time job to become a health coach.
Eager to make her dreams a reality, she quit her job in Boston,
moved to San Francisco, and started looking for clients. She
thought that because she was so jazzed about coaching, and rent
in San Francisco at that time was lower than rents in Boston, she
had all she needed to succeed.

What Kristen didn't have was financial ground underneath
her to cover her basic life expenses. She had no wiggle room.
And she also had nothing to help her develop her business. It
was a direct line to debt and difficulty. "I struggled more than

I needed to that first year because I didn't set myself up with a bridge job. I barely made enough from my new clients to cover groceries, rent, and public transport."

In hindsight, Kristen wished she'd had a job that had covered her basics while her enterprise got up and running. "Because you need to invest in your own education, marketing, and team in order to grow your business. Building a website does not a business make." Without enough financial support, you slow down the growth of your new business. According to Kristen, even with six months to a year's worth of savings, a bridge job is essential.

You want something completely the opposite of your business. Steady and boring. You don't want to hustle to find clients—so nothing like yoga teaching or sales. You don't want unpredictable hours—so think twice about waitressing or other shift work. You don't want to wonder when you'll get paid. Slow and steady is best. Think easy desk job. "The best bridge jobs are the ones you're overqualified for and bored doing," Kristen says. You don't have to prove your education, skills, or experience all the time. Save that for building your business. Believe me, you'll be glad you did.

PART 3

Your Terms: Mastering Cash Flow

Save your money, save the world.

CHAPTER 9

Wings.

Create affluence on any income.

I n this section, we move from roots to wings. Wings provide your day-to-day cash flow, whether by income or savings. Your wings plant your garden and water your roots. Your wings are strongest when you earn more than you spend, so that you can fatten your savings without leaning heavily on credit.

Cash can spring from a variety of sources: a full-time or part-time job, an emergency fund, credit card, real estate rentals, or even Mom and Dad. Here, we focus on three sources: your professional income, savings account, and credit.

Please note that in this book I covered roots first, and then wings. That's intentional. If you aim to budget first, save second, and invest third, it's hard to ensure you'll have enough cash to fund your future when it's last in line. Instead, I hope you now think about your roots first, and then create a spending plan that enables you to grow them.

In an ideal month, you earn more than you spend. In reality, the earning-spending ride is full of ups and downs, credits and debts, windfalls and shortfalls. Your goal is positive net worth so that you have equity and income now and later. Your personal choices directly impact your prosperity, and we're all better for it. But you don't just wake up with positive net worth. Life is full of curveballs, and WHAM, your income evaporates, your credit card balance balloons, and the real estate market tanks. You're slogging through a muddy bog of tuition bills and debt payments. It's a seesaw of ups and downs. Or a hamster wheel.

Ah, budgets, the holy grail of personal finance. We will address budgeting through a framework called *money clarity* in chapter eleven. In the meantime, remember that your spending strategy is as much about debt protection as it is about funding assets.

If I've made any of this book feel like a diet prescription, I've failed. If you're nervous about reading yet another budgeting tip you can't keep, don't fret. These next few chapters aren't about generating a robotic level of willpower or denying you pleasure. They're about how to navigate the daily push and pull of income, saving, and spending.

When it comes to my business, I use two methods: "top-down" and "bottom-up" planning. Top-down planning looks at business budgeting through a lens of revenue goals. For example, if we spend more on marketing, how much more revenue can we make? Top-down planning is expansive and flexible. Bottom-up planning is austere, beginning with existing cash balances and contractually booked income. Personal budgeting works more like bottom-up planning. It's fixed. In my experience, it takes just as much effort to increase income as it does to cut expenses, so I will try to elaborate more on top-down planning.

Imagine you could snap your fingers and magically widen

the gap between your income and your spending. Tomorrow, you walk into your office, demand (and get!) a raise, while simultaneously selling your house and moving back in with your parents. More money, less overhead! It's a miracle. Granted, that scenario's unlikely, but I bet I've sparked your interest. Let's explore some more realistic strategies for earning more and spending less on big things—top-down.

Is Your Income Competitive and Consistent?

Have you checked lately to see if you're earning within the appropriate range for your career and city? According to Glass door.com, a director of development (nonprofit fund-raiser) living in Philadelphia earns, on average, $86,000 a year. A copywriter in Los Angeles earns $45,000. If your earnings are significantly out of line with others in your industry, you could be underearning for the simple reason that you didn't know you should be earning more based on what others like you now earn. As we've already covered here, as has every women's magazine ad nauseam, women are more likely to earn less than men in the same job. Don't be a statistic. Find out if you're underearning, and either ask for a raise or begin your job search. You're not a charity.

Jill Davi decided to face her situation. "I sat down and figured out how much I was spending in relation to what I was making. It was clear I was a classic underearner. I was using credit cards to float my lifestyle and was too nervous to ask for a raise or search for a better job. I realized I had to cut back on spending, but I also needed to get a higher-paying job. I knew

I was doing more than my share of the work and not getting paid accordingly and was feeling resentful: I received praise and recognition, but not an increase or a promotion. So I decided to look outside the company for other opportunities. I found a higher-paying job with a promotion, at a company that paid all my benefits and had a generous bonus structure. It came at the perfect time."

In addition to maximizing your earning, you also need consistent income. Easier said than done if you're a stubborn entrepreneur like me. Fluctuating income makes planning very difficult.

As a business owner, even if you're a solopreneur (no employees), deposit all business income into a dedicated business checking account. Then transfer a fixed monthly paycheck to your personal checking account. Accountants refer to this process as a "draw." Yes, this means leaving cash in your business bank account even when you've got hungry, graspy hands claiming those dollars (like personal credit cards).

If you always pay yourself everything your business earns, you're adding business instability to your personal instability. Put yourself on a fixed draw and retain your bonuses for annual payouts when you can assess twelve-month business income history.

No matter how you earn, whether freelance or full-time, never reject money that's rightfully yours. Last week, as I calculated the weekly pay I owed to our babysitter, Jenna, I asked her: "Didn't you buy my kids dinner last week? How much was that?" I also offered to pay her for gasoline. She said, "Don't worry about it." I had to insist. Like so many women, she wants to be liked, not a drain or a nuisance. But in doing so, she had voluntarily sacrificed $40 against her $200 weekly income—20 percent. Are you doing some version of the same? Take money when it's offered, especially when the provider is a professional superior or someone you know can damn well afford it!

Remember that income serves two purposes: paying for today while investing in roots for tomorrow. Don't forget.

Is Your Overhead Low?

At twelve years old, I remember sleeping over at my friend's pristine, colonnaded McMansion. The buzz-cut lawn resembled AstroTurf, the backyard play set was its own fairy-tale castle, and inside, the white carpets stretched on like heavenly clouds. When my aunt picked me up the following day, she asked me, "Did you notice there's barely any furniture and no art on the walls?" I hadn't noticed, but I got what she was saying. They hadn't just moved in; they were house poor. They were likely spending so much on their mortgage (and lawn) that there was nothing left for furniture.

In greatest service to yourself and your loved ones, don't live within your means, live as far below your means as you can. It's the only way to create affluence. There will always be opportunities to travel, take vacations, boost your retirement, help a friend in need. Once you've locked yourself into a home, car, or annual contract of any form, reducing any overhead could be hard and expensive. Your cash is committed.

How are you doing now? Assess whether your monthly home-related costs, including all the extras (utilities, lawn mowing, etc.), costs 30 percent or less than your monthly net income. If you live in New York City, you may be spending up to 50 percent. No matter what, less overhead means more choices.

Are You Spending with Intention?

Listen, I know how powerful it feels to wear a tailored black designer suit to a sales pitch, the pleasure of wrapping myself in cashmere on a cold day, the pride of carpooling kids in a shiny SUV, and the joy of giving gifts. But your professional success is not contingent upon your wardrobe; you already own many beautiful sweaters, kids fit in many modes of transport, and your cousin already owned the Keurig you bought him for Christmas. If you're carrying debt or are unable to save, stop the madness.

Ask what purchases really make you happy, and which ones only do because you think they should? Are you spending to make other people happy, like your parents? Is it working? Reflect.

If you want to fund real roots (which require extra cash), you have to carefully select a few indulgences and slash the rest. This point is so important that I've dedicated a later chapter to it.

Stand for Substance

It's Sunday, September 25, and it finally feels like autumn, as we're released from the unrelenting heat of summer. Today is the Chestnut Hill Fall for the Arts, my Philadelphia neighborhood street fair. My kids dress in brightly colored T-shirts so that I can spot them in the crowd.

I withdraw $200 from the ATM in anticipation of buying a rustic wooden vanity to replace the crumbling IKEA desk in my bedroom. Spending money on locally crafted wares not only enriches my life, it fuels our local economy. We connect to how our dollars nourish and sustain our neighbors' livelihoods. We can, in some cases, learn about how the products were manufactured and what materials were used, and witness the passion that went into building them.

Spending can be joyful when it seeds and supports communities and businesses that sustain our lives. But too often every expense we face can be accompanied by guilt and anxiety. Read any finance book you want: our individual capacity to discern between needs and wants can feel impossible inside of our broader cultural addiction to buying our way through periods of boredom, family expectations, or who knows what holiday.

Affluenza: The All-Consuming Epidemic by John de Graaf, David Wann, and Thomas Naylor illustrates in detail the crushing personal and social impact of out-of-control spending. Affluenza, as they've named it, is "a painful, contagious socially transmitted condition of overload, debt, anxiety, and waste resulting from the dogged pursuit of more." They explain, "the affluenza epidemic is rooted in the obsessive, almost religious quest for economic expansion that has become the core principle of what is called the American Dream." Affluenza's ultimate threat? To exhaust our individual financial security along with the Earth's resources. John, David, and Thomas: we hear you, and we know. We all know we need to shift this dynamic, for our planet and ourselves.

Of course, your thinking and behavior with money will naturally influence those around you. And, if you have kids, you are creating indelible imprints that will serve them for their entire lives. Karla Trotman, who runs a business supporting women before and after pregnancy, was at lunch recently with her mother and two-year-old son. When the bill came, her son produced her debit card to pay. "I realized he thought that card was magic. I needed to set him up to understand the full cycle, the part where you *pay off* the bill." She now tells her kids that if they want something, they have to pay for it. Together they make a plan for how that will happen. "As parents, we shield them from a lot. But they need to think about money in a real-life way," she said. "It's not too early to start."

Easier stated than implemented. We're caught in a loop of binge and purge. Consider the boggling success of the Kon-Mari technique, a book bought by millions of people, including myself. Tokyo-based personal organizer Marie Kondo's housekeeping manual, *The Life-Changing Magic of Tidying Up: The Japanese Art of Decluttering and Organizing*, sold more than two million copies in less than six months after its US publication in October 2014. The author's name has become fused to the zeitgeist, with people now deploying *Kondo* as a verb to describe deep-sixing their bloated closets and drawers. In her book, Kondo is Zen-like, downright spiritual, insisting that joy is key to the downsizing process. By surrounding yourself only with things you love, you are always reminded of who you are and what you care about.

Smart spending is as much about personal sustainability as it is about breaking our cultural obsession with buying, immediate satisfaction, and entitlement. You work hard for your income, but are you exerting the same level of passion and energy into your own health and well-being? I'm not saying this is easy. I'm just asking you to step back and ask: why?

On deck next: Kondo-ing our consumption. Our current rate is neither desirable nor necessary.

CHAPTER 10

Overcoming Overspending.

You didn't really want it in the first place.

S pending can be joyful when it's done intentionally, but you
need a strategy for the moments when you're unconscious.
Being a money manager means going to Target prepared! I'm
not talking about austerity. I'm not against spending, or the
thrill of buying. I just want you to explore your habits in more
depth. When you spend with intention, I hope you'll buy less
and save more.

Let's have some fun, shall we? I have a series of challenges
for you.

These experiments aren't designed to reactivate your money
story. When you hit those ouchy bumps—and you will—
observe, breathe, and keep going. Don't indulge the drama.
By the end of these exercises, you will have a very good idea of
where all that money goes and how to make mindful changes to
your spending.

Ready to play?

Challenge #1: Cut It Out

Log in and read through at least one full month of credit card and bank account statements. Find one recurring charge that you no longer use or need, such as a subscription or a membership. Then cancel it.

Figure out how much money you just saved this month (an $18 subscription) and move $18 into your savings account. Good work, saver.

Challenge #2: What Did You Buy in the Past Three Days?

From memory first, think about where you've been the last three days. Did you drive anywhere or take the train? Were you at work, with kids, friends, or family? Did you eat at home or at a restaurant?

Write down what you bought and how much it cost (exclude fixed expenses like bills). Don't get lost in the rabbit hole of analysis. Include food, groceries, transportation, a pack of gum, emergency mascara, new sunglasses because you left yours on the train, iTunes or Amazon purchases.

Now, log in to your accounts and see how close you are to what you wrote down from memory. What have you learned about how much you spend and why?

It's enlightening to see where your money goes. When you write down what you spend, you start to see how often you spend on impulse. Who are you as a spender? That's what we're investigating. It's a key exercise that gives you deeper insights into your own habits and mind-set around spending.

Remember, Money Buddhas don't judge. They just observe. Humans have known for thousands of years that material gain does not create happiness. Austerity doesn't, either. Padded savings accounts? Ecstasy. I swear.

Shopping Therapy: Not Therapeutic

If you've ever shopped to make yourself feel better, you are not alone. Both men and women do it. Spending money is immediate and gratifying. It's an easy way to compensate for short-term irritations and disappointments. Crappy morning getting out of the house on time? There's a nice hot beverage waiting for you at Starbucks, and then a new travel mug. $15 gone, and within a month, $150.

Everyday stressors can send anyone into retail land for that crucial dopamine boost. But for women, this dangerous remedy is especially tricky. Studies show that women spend money to help them regulate emotions more than men. In 2014, Dr. Karen Pine, a psychologist at the University of Hertfordshire, surveyed seven hundred women about their tendency to indulge in retail therapy. Turns out that women shop a lot more when their emotions—whether positive or negative—are running high. No matter that they are already worrying about not having enough money. In the moment, it feels so good to buy something that we briefly forget that we are already carrying a hefty credit card balance—maybe one that we can't pay off every month. Or that we have zero savings. The pleasure feels unrelated to the anxiety. Yet more than half of the women in Dr. Pine's study said they would gladly give up shopping if they could find another, more reliable way of relieving their angst.

Falling for It

Get real about where you lack control—if you do. When you go to the grocery store—or to Target, or to Amazon.com—do you buy five things that weren't on your list? Do you make a list? Flag that as a problem area. No judgment, just see it.

We often buy for reasons that have nothing to do with what we need. Why? The thrill of spending money temporarily soothes those uncomfortable feelings. We overspend due to boredom, anxiety, or stress. The thing is: spending unconsciously undermines your power.

Marketers know that people shop to fill emotional voids and are amazing at getting your money out of your hands and into theirs. They convince you that you'll be happier, freer, and more liked by others when you own their products. And you're falling for it. We all do, to some extent. Are you going to let someone else's strategy for making money ruin your credit?

Challenge #3: Spend-Free Weekend

This weekend or next, plan to go spend-free. From Friday at five p.m. to Sunday at four p.m., eat the food you have while doing things that don't cost money. It's not a punishment—it's an experiment, and one that opens up deep awareness around our spending addictions. Consider enrolling your family in the game, or teaming up with a friend and doing it together. Remember, it's not forever! It's just a weekend. If your inner rebel is currently screaming, No *way*! keep reading. You may choose to play anyway.

Treat it like a game. If you're hosting guests or already have plans that require spending, isolate those events and spend that cash guilt-free. But don't use those events as excuses to throw away the entire assignment. Rarely do we have the chance to see our lives highlighted in this way. Just like when you go on a juice fast or a cleanse, you get to see yourself through the lens of what's missing. What do you crave? How important is that thing to your long-term well-being and happiness? If it was Doritos or Twinkies, it would be easy to identify—even if the habit was not as easy to change. When it's dropping fifteen dollars on lunch every day (four dollars of that on a drink), it can be harder to see.

The spend-free weekend is a detox from spending. I know this is a big one, but it's worth any discomfort you might experience. Remember, it's temporary, and no one is going to scold you if you don't do it perfectly. Certainly not me. I just want you to get a good, long look at what you tend to do.

Ready? Here goes: Don't spend any money this weekend. Nothing. Nada. Zero. This is an entirely new challenge. By not spending at all, you'll start to see what the biggest obstacles are between you and clarity.

Here are ten guidelines to support you:

1. **Treat it like a game.** This is key. It's the secret to making this fun! Experiment. Take the pressure off. See how you do.

2. **Don't freak out, feel guilty, or shame yourself if you do spend money.** That's not the point. I'm not testing you. I'm asking you to discover new ways of occupying your free time that don't involve amassing new stuff.

3. **Be intentional about your spend-free parameters.** For example, "I will not spend money starting on Saturday at ten a.m., and I'll stop on Sunday at two p.m." Believe me,

within those parameters—even if you stop by the grocery store first and head right to the bar after—you will have insights about your habits. You are in charge of drawing your own boundaries.

4. **Push your creativity.** If you're about to do something that costs money, first stop and ask: is there another way?

5. **Find joy in free activities.** Notice how often we spend money to relieve anxiety or boredom. Start to trip that wire and pause that habit.

6. **Resist temptation.** If you really need something (my car is out of gas!), buy gas. Don't deny your baby formula. Just don't buy anything else. Bring a one-item list if you need to. It's not ridiculous—it's a strategy.

7. **Be gentle.** If you do end up spending money you didn't intend to spend, forgive yourself, brush it off, and try again.

8. **Allow for humanity.** If you're finding this assignment impossible this weekend, try to have a spend-free day instead. Or plan for another weekend. There is no detention.

9. **Have fun!** There's a beautiful world out there. This is a perfect excuse to rediscover it.

10. **Track it!** Keep tabs on exactly how much money you are saving. Make a list—on your phone, a scrap of paper, etc. When the weekend is over, move that exact amount—what you would have spent during a typical weekend (estimate as best you can)—into your savings account.

I can't help but laugh when I entertain a spend-free weekend, even though I've done it ten times now. It's scary when you think about it. What if I NEED something? As you go through the weekend, write about what's surprising you and what you are learning about yourself. That's where the juice is. Don't keep it to yourself.

It Was Radical

When Kadine Niedermeyer did the spend-free-weekend exercise, she was just beginning to find her way around the basics of money, tracking her income and expenses, setting up the right accounts. Kadine had been in arts school when the 2008 recession hit, and after college she'd moved in with her fiancé to save money. But rents in Seattle are high, and as a junior interior decorator, she had a hard time finding full-time work. Plus, she had no idea how to prioritize the money she did have.

The exercise was eye-opening. What she didn't realize before she took the challenge was that for her, the act of spending money had a really fundamental value. In her mind, it was the *same* as being alive. So at first, even the *idea* of not spending money for two days was nerve-wracking. "I thought I was going to die—I thought, You mean, I can't spend even a dollar?!? It was scary," she says. "But the reality was that I had a great, relaxing weekend. I didn't have to worry about spending money. I was fine, and that was a revelation: if you don't need anything, don't buy anything. Now it seems silly, but at the moment it was radical."

That's enough games for now. There's more to say about spending.

A Lot to Do with Our Relationships

Now, you might be thinking, *I'm not a shopper. I'm as frugal as my great-grandmother was under the Russian tsar.* But even you, dear reader, may have either regretted buying something (those two-for-one spring boots?), or spent more than you could afford at some point (that outdoor gas grill?), for reasons that you can't easily justify. Binge shopping or just overspending also have a lot to do with our relationships. Women tend to buy for others, either to treat them, to take care of them, or to impress them. It also has to do with how we believe we want to see ourselves. Sometimes we're trying to spend our way to a new identity. The thinking (which might be unconscious) is, *If I become a chef, a tennis player, or a Sunday painter, then I will be happy and loved.* We buy lots of gear to support this new identity. But rarely do we end up using it.

For me, it is usually around the kitchen. I'll buy the fancy food processor, the cookie baking trays, and the cookbooks. Then, of course, my kitchen needs a nice rug because I'll be standing by the stove a lot more. None of this cooking and baking actually happens. But I will go to IKEA five times to get everything. And then my house is full of baking gear that I've never used. This is not a great way to live.

Researchers have long known about the impact on our identities of making purchases. Russell Belk, a pioneering marketing researcher at York University in Toronto, has found that we shop our way into or out of identities. Shopping helps us feel like we belong to a certain group—or don't belong. When do we most want to be someone else? When we're bored, stressed, or anxious. We shop to get out of the house or office, to distract ourselves—and sometimes to get out of our own skin. Think about how some people going through divorce change their look completely—new clothes, accessories, and hairstyle—to signal their new selves. If our purchases have a lasting impact on our joy, then they are more justifiable. But most of the time, this kind of purchasing just gets us into trouble. The shopping high comes to an abrupt end when the shoes don't really fit, the tennis racket stays stashed, the easel is folded up in the corner. And then your credit card bill comes.

Bright, Shiny Objects

There are also social conventions that pressure us to buy when we don't really need to. Some of that just has to do with wanting—or being told that we need something new to fit the occasion. Most people experience a jolt of happiness or pleasure when we acquire something new or different, say researchers at Tufts University. Even kids know this, and that's why they clamor for new stuff in September, making back-to-school an expensive time of the year. So are kids' birthdays, the change of the seasons, vacations, weddings, dinner parties. You think you need to bring a fancy gift, or buy new outfits, or impress your dinner guests with new furniture or cookware.

Your kids may think this, too. After making this mistake too many times, I now buy my kids only two new things in the fall, while reusing most of their school supplies and binders from last year. They're mostly in fine condition. No new backpacks or lunch boxes unless their existing ones are broken and beyond repair. When I feel the pressure to buy, I have to slow down and ask, *Does this really matter, or am I just trying to fit in?* At age thirty-nine, I'm no longer concerned with fitting in (whatever "in" means anyway), so why would I spend money to soothe latent insecurities? Do I genuinely desire to give this gift, or am I buying it because I remember various guilt trips for being "unthoughtful"? Do I know what that person wants or am I just anticipating fear of seeming unloving? Do I care about how people perceive the material value of the gift, or is a beautiful, handwritten card or a bouquet of flowers enough to express my love? Once I've reflected, I usually send flowers.

Getting mindful about what you spend—and how you spend—isn't about taming every impulse. It's about strategies.

When Stephanie Licata was a freelancer, she preferred to work around other people, not alone at home in her pajamas. This drove her to spend more money than she wanted to. "I started to notice how much I spent on meals out—even casual or small ones." She caught herself overspending to compensate for her feelings of isolation. But once she saw what she'd been doing—unconsciously—she created a strategy for herself that allows her to save money *and* be around people. "Now, on the days I work from home, I cook and prepare food. And if I go out to Panera or Starbucks, I give myself a limit on how much I can spend. I also started going to my local library and started using my alum card to go to the university library more so I am not in places where I will spend money, but I am still getting out with people. The upside? I have lost six pounds since I started tracking my spending because I am more conscious of the food I am eating, too."

Here are some more shopping tips from Dr. Karen Pine, who has studied the behavior and psychology of women and spending (check out www.sheconomics.com for more from Dr. Pine):

1. **Spend only cash.** Leave your debit and credit cards somewhere else, out of reach. This automatically puts a limit on your spending and keeps impulse buys contained.

2. **Shop alone.** Shopping with friends can bring on peer pressure, even subtly. Shop alone or choose to go with someone thriftier than you.

3. **Change *when* you shop.** If you always shop on Fridays after work or Saturday afternoons, fill that time with other fun things that don't involve spending money. Change your reflexive habits. Shake 'em up. You might not need to shop after all.

4. **Keep purchases small.** If you must buy something to ease the angst, make it small (and nonedible)—a modest bouquet of flowers, a magazine, a new lipstick.

5. **Don't shop "hangry."** If you're hungry or angry ("hangry"), avoid shopping altogether. Same goes for when you're tired or upset. Get some food or some sleep, talk to a trusted friend or counselor, and save the shopping for when you feel more on an even keel.

It takes some practice, but clear strategies to keep spending at bay will make the buying you do more pleasurable (no angst!). If you can slow down enough to appreciate what you're buying, you'll enjoy the object more when you bring it home.

I'm challenging you to look at very personal habits that you have most likely been glossing over. It's normal. We all do it. But you might be a little bewildered by how you truly spend your money. The next time you find yourself engaged in retail therapy—or contemplating it—stop and think: What's a real need here and what's not real? Is there something soothing I can do for myself that does not involve spending money? Worst-case scenario, put things in your cart, but don't press buy. Not just yet. Leave your (real or virtual) cart by the door for now.

Remember, just because you buy something on sale or opt not to grab a magazine at checkout doesn't mean you've saved any money. When you do forgo an impulse buy, transfer what you didn't spend out of checking and into your savings account. It's not savings until you do. Watching your savings grow can be more exhilarating than impulse spending. I promise.

That's Not Negotiable

I bought my first house without any real understanding of what we could afford because it fit a vision of what I aspired to. Had I known the headaches it would cause, I'd have gladly bought a house a few blocks away, half the size, for half the cost. Upon deeper reflection, I now know I have a handful of "nonnegotiables." My four nonnegotiables include: private school for my kids, an annual trip abroad with my kids, a weekly dinner out, and a housekeeper twice per month. Every other material object I can take or leave, or use what I already own.

Otherwise, I rent a small house, buy only classic work suits and boots that I wear for three to five years at a time, and cut and dye my own hair. When I leave behind the things I don't really care about, I can save real sums of money. And that's what freedom means to me. Cash when I need it. When the good money you earn evaporates over and over again, saving becomes a desirable goal in and of itself.

Your four nonnegotiables are not the same as mine, but they have the same aim: spend some money on what you love, save the rest. What are *yours*?

Zero in on **four areas** of spending that you absolutely cannot do without. These could be big or small. Maybe it's shoes or clothes, eating lunch out during the workweek, or leasing a new car. Because to *not* do these things would feel restrictive, austere, and irritating, and make you want to quit managing your money altogether. Move those aside. We won't touch those.

When you look at how much you spend on negotiables—the things you don't care about as much—what could you be saving? We want exact numbers here.

A National Scale

In 2013, middle-class American households were carrying an average of $15,000 in credit card debt and paid $2,500 a year in interest! It may be tempting to blame our culture, but the reality is far more complex. Since 2003, household income has grown 26 percent, but the cost of living has risen 29 percent. Household debt has grown 15 percent faster than household income. Medical costs have grown 51 percent. Food and beverage costs have grown 37 percent.

Add on medical bills, the cost of college, or living in an expensive city, and you're another stat in stagnation: an educated professional with a good job and credible résumé not making ends meet.

Decide Where Credit Is Due

It's so easy to overspend, overborrow, and lean on credit cards when we need to. Too easy. If credit card debt is your norm, then it's time to face it like a boss. Debt in general is not bad. It's just expensive, especially when you're accruing it to buy things you didn't really want in the first place.

Do you ever just stash that credit card bill, close that screen, and then throw some money at your statement at another date, only to charge the same amount or more to your credit card the very next day? Or you slide deeper into your money story: *I can't, it's too hard, what's the point?* And sometimes you inherit debt. Your ex blew up your business. You inherited your spouse's debt when you divorced. It's really not fair. And yet the mess is yours. Sometimes not knowing how to wrangle debt is linked to simply not knowing how credit works.

Debt is a window into our lives' curveballs or blind spots. Credit cards, like the twenty half-mangled Barbies on my living room floor, are like plastic playthings. The cause-and-effect relationship has evaporated. If you've ever worked in a cash industry—such as waitressing—where you leave your shift with cash in your hands, you can feel the direct relationship between the work you do and the buying power you have. With cash, you viscerally experience where your money goes. With credit cards, that direct relationship does not exist.

If you have too much debt, here are a few ways to wrangle it.

Hit It All At Once

In 2005, when Sylvia Flores's career as a creative director suddenly got traction, she enjoyed everything money could buy. Credit card companies were freely extending attractive offers, especially since Flores had a more than $250,000 annual salary. "It was a lot like Monopoly money," she says. "I got the giant house, the great cars, the beautiful clothes, and it was all on credit—to the tune of about $500,000." But, in the way of money, a whole bunch of tough expenses hit at once. The housing market crashed, and America went into a stark depression. Flores got hit with unexpected medical bills, and at the same time she got divorced. "I was paying out 50 percent of my income to my ex, while I also assumed 100 percent of our debt. Ouch." She went from smooth sailing to hitting an iceberg. Flores did what I caution against, though it happens: she used her 401(k) and IRA to pay off $440,000 of her debt. She still had $120,000 in debt left, as well as taxes to pay.

Sylvia's debt level was profound. You may not have $560,000 in debt, but you may have more than is easy to pay off. While Sylvia's situation is not unusual, it's entirely normal. As Dave Ramsey says, "Debt is normal. Be weird."

A Logical Crutch

I mentioned Jill Davi earlier. Here's more about her: She earned less than $30,000 a year as an entry-level assistant in television. She lived in an expensive city (New York) and liked to go out with friends for drinks and to see shows. It's fine to enjoy your twenties in an exciting city—I did it, too—the problem was that most of Jill's salary went toward rent, leaving little to spare. Credit cards seemed like a logical crutch. Her wake-up call happened when creditors started calling. Consider that her forced money coma awakening. She was in too deep to climb out. Between three credit cards and a personal loan, her debt was now higher than her $30,000 annual salary. Like so many people, she had been trying to ignore it.

Despite her unconscious spending, Jill is a principled person. Sick and angry that she was in so much trouble, one night she had a reckoning with herself. She did not want to declare bankruptcy. She looked at herself in the mirror and harnessed her anger to take control. "Suddenly, I was determined, resolute, and scared as hell. I cut up all my cards, except the one my parents had opened for me in college. I put that one in a Tupperware container filled with water, and stuck it in the freezer, so I couldn't use it," she says.

Jill and Sylvia, though at very different points in their careers, had similar problems. They vastly underestimated their debt and their ability to manage it. This is normal. According to a study commissioned by NerdWallet, a site dedicated to advising consumers about the good and the bad of credit, in 2013 what individuals reported they owed was 155 percent lower than what they actually owed. That means that we are 155 percent likely to underestimate how much trouble we are in. If you're the exception here, thank you. You carry the torch—let it shine.

Thanks, Client #0003067842

Here's how credit works. Banks and credit card companies are businesses. They are like ExxonMobil or Safeway or Nike. They have a brand, they want to attract your business, and they offer you services and incentives because they need to make money. This may sound obvious, but it's worth stating clearly: your lenders want to *make* money. They are not like libraries, promoting knowledge and well-being in the greater society. They are businesses. Lenders (banks, credit cards, student loan institutions, etc.) earn on interest on loans or other debt products. If the bank gives you 1 percent interest on the $1,000 in your savings account ($10/year), but makes 5 percent interest on the HELOC (home equity line of credit) you took out to remodel your kitchen ($5,000/year), they win. You are paying them 4 percent more than what you earned. Thanks, client #0003067842.

But credit is not *bad*. It's just that in the last thirty years, it's become way easier to get credit. The Silent Generation (born between 1928 and 1945) rejected it more so than the generations that followed. They could live *only* within their means. Imagine that. Baby Boomers and Gen Xers grew up with restricted credit access, but then in the mid-'80s and early '90s had sudden access to lots of it.

The credit system has advantages (perks, rewards, and protections) and disadvantages (rapacious interest rates, penalizing fees). There's an upside and a downside. Get the game before the game gets you. These days, if you are going to live on the grid in North America, you need a credit score. If you want to buy a car or a house, you will need to show your creditworthiness. To do so, you need a credit history—evidence that you're a secure borrower and successful at paying it back. Having credit not only allows you to pay for things that you don't have enough money for today, but also gives you the ability to borrow more later. A good credit score reduces the interest you pay. The better you are at paying back loans, the lower your rates will be in the future.

Credit helps. And you need to handle it with great scrutiny and care. When you have good credit, you may qualify for better interest rates—with big debts like mortgages, HELOCs, and car loans, lower APRs can save you thousands of dollars. You can take advantage of better rewards and protections. Credit cards will extend warranties on many products, as well as give you collision insurance on rental cars, and money back and points on shopping or travel. You may get lower fees, or no fees, on loan products. You may have fewer obstacles when qualifying for rental apartments, mortgages, or cars.

Good credit means your debt costs you less to carry. If you have a good credit score (700+), you'll have an easier time reducing existing interest on your loans. For example, on $20,000 of credit card debt, if you are paying 7 percent in interest rather than 23 percent, you will pay a lot less every month—to the tune of about $266/mo. Multiply this over twelve months and you are saving over $3,000 a year. That's a lot. This goes for mortgages and car payments, too.

Bad Debt Just Means It's Expensive

People talk about good and bad debt. If your debt enables you to build clear roots, then your debt may be a risk-worthy investment. If your debt funds depreciating assets—like clothes you'll wear out in a single season—you're not aware of the game that's playing you. So you see what's going on here? Credit is not free money until you can use it to your advantage.

In 2013, after years of no balance, I woke up to $6,000 of credit card debt I'd been carrying for four months. Imagine I had to pay $2,634 as interest charges over ten years, but invested the money instead. Say I earn 5 percent interest compounded annually. After ten years, I'd have $4,290. You get it. I know, easy for me to say. But what an opportunity cost!

If you're thinking *Amanda Steinberg is the Zen Buddha of debt management—I bet she always pays off her cards in the 'right way,'* I don't. I have to regenerate my willpower and stare down my demons over and over. When I finally faced the medical bills on my credit card—which I'd been avoiding for two months— my solar plexus burned with anticipation. My stomach muscles clenched. Upon sitting down at my computer, I stopped breathing for a minute as I debated whether to check Twitter one more time or log in to my Chase account.

If you have *a lot* of credit card debt, I won't lie to you: you're in need of some significant changes. Whether you need to change your career or restructure your overhead, there's always a way, you just might not like it. Don't count on any rescue fantasy that you're not in direct control of manifesting. For example, my friend Mary married an investment banker only to learn post-nuptials that he was hundreds of thousands of dollars in debt. And Elizabeth believed she'd be inheriting over $1 million from her father when he died. He left her nothing.

Planning is not a bad word. It's an excuse to reinvent areas of your life that aren't working. An opportunity to quit doing things that no longer serve you.

I Am Free!

Being an optimist, Sylvia Flores started her financial life again from scratch. She decided not to make too much of a big deal about what it would take to pay down her $120,000. "I came from very humble, do-it-yourself beginnings on a farm, so I knew I could get back to the basics. I just had to remind myself that the frugal life can also be a fun and creative life." Setting up a spreadsheet, Flores decided what to pay month by month, how much she could afford, and when she would be clear of the mess.

"I learned how extremely gratifying it is to highlight a row in red and mark it PAID. I made sure not to delete these paid lines, ever. It was a game: once the spreadsheet was one hundred percent highlighted, I realized, I am FREE!"

Good Credit Card Habits

1. **Pay on time.** Thirty-five percent of your credit score comes from on-time payment. With automatic minimum payments, it's a relatively easy win.

2. **Never charge more than you can pay off in four months.** The ideal is to pay off your entire balance every month, but for many people, that's not realistic.

3. **That said, pay *at least* double your minimum payment** every month. By exceeding your minimum payments, you will exponentially decrease the cost of interest.

4. **Be conservative.** It's ideal to have two personal cards. Do not have more than five or you may be flagged as potentially untrustworthy by lenders—someone who might be in trouble and unable to pay back their loans. Not to mention that it will be almost impossible to track your spending if you have that many cards open.

5. **Keep an eye on your long-term dreams** and prioritize from there. Do you want to qualify for a mortgage? Go on a vacation you can afford? Remember, credit card companies want your money. And you aren't in the game to increase AMEX's profit margin. You're here to live the life you want. So focus on that. Don't be fabulous at the expense of real integrity.

Score!

Your credit history is all the information ever filed about money that you've borrowed, either as loans or credit cards, and how you pay your bills. This information goes on your *credit report*,

and you are given a *credit score*, a number between 300 and 850—
the higher the better.

Your credit score (also known as your FICO score) is
based on:

- 35 percent payment history (Do you pay on time?)
- 30 percent of the amount you currently owe (Are you close
  to maxing out?)
- 15 percent length of credit history (How long have you
  been borrowing money for?)
- 10 percent new credit (older accounts and a variety of accounts are best)
- 10 percent type of credit used (How diversified are your
  sources of credit?)

To find your credit score, I recommend www.creditkarma.com.

Moonlighting

Really think hard about how you can pay down your cards. Do
you need an extra job just for this purpose? Make it temporary,
but make it happen. Make sure, if you're not accustomed to freelance income, to save 30 percent toward taxes. If you don't, you'll
get a surprise unhappy bill from the IRS that could send you
back into debt.

If I'm losing you in these details, just keep reading. Rome
wasn't built in a day, as the saying goes. You can come back to
these tips later. Learning the language and the strategies will
begin to have a measurable impact on your bottom line.

Here's a money mantra to repeat when you start to doubt yourself—or anytime.

> *Money gives me choices.*
> *Even when life throws curveballs,*
> *I don't believe "I'm bad with money."*
> *Ups and downs are part of the journey.*
> *I fund my own security and freedom*
> *by spending and saving consciously every day.*
> *It's* worth it.

Now that you have a new handle on earning, spending, and credit, we're going to get really serious about saving. It's all about to come together, like magic. Saving is the fire in your volcano. Saving keeps you out of debt and funds your roots. Saving is the secret weapon in your net worth.

CHAPTER 11

Money Clarity.

From chaos to clarity.

A ccording to a 2014 Gallup poll, only 30 percent of Americans are successful at budgeting. That makes 70 percent of them *unsuccessful.* Why? Fluctuating bills, unexpected crises, major life changes—and the reality that most human brains are not primed to track five hundred distinct transactions per month and tuck them into neat, clearly delineated categories. In my opinion, 70 percent means that for most people, budgeting does not work. As soon as you begin, you can't stay within the parameters you've set for yourself. You feel like a failure.

If you're one of 30 percent of Americans who successfully stick to a budget and pay your credit cards every month, keep doing what you're doing. If you're not, I've created a different method, a modification to the personal finance system known as "bucketing." It's called *money clarity*, and it begins when you assign real numbers to the following major categories.

Write down your numbers in the margins of this book if that's helpful.

You can choose how to work through these exercises, but no

matter what, make sure it contains "money in" and "money out." What net earnings come in monthly? What expenses must go out?

Even small steps like logging into bank accounts can drive anyone ape shit. I need my username. Now I need my password. I'm waiting for my verification code. It's not here. Special security question? I filled this out three years ago. I don't know the color of my childhood car's interior. I was four years old. I'd rather be cleaning out my fridge or catching up on episodes of *The Americans*. You have to be kidding me.

Okay, enough. Remember: Video games. Gold coins.

Depending on how organized you already are, reviewing your bank statements could be fast and easy—or it could take some time. You might review your statements regularly, or you might not have checked in for quite a while. Do *not* judge yourself for your past behavior. We've released shame, and we're playing a game. The fact that you are reading this far means you're beyond self-sabotage. With access to your accounts and a summary of what you have, we move on.

Money In, Money Out

Feeling in control of your finances begins with the sheer thrill of knowing how much you have to work with each month. Is your bottom line positive or negative? We're going to start with money in (income), and then we'll move on to what goes out (save, sustain, and spend) and put it together to see what's really going on.

Money in: How much income do you NET every month, after taxes?

Attention All Freelancers! If you are self-employed, do not
include the percentage of income that you owe in taxes as
income. This is so important! Making this mistake can
destroy your best attempts at earning. You think you have
money, but—oops!—you actually owe it to the government.

Money out: save + sustain + spend

Save: How much can you afford to contribute to your emergency, curveball (more on this later), and retirement funds
every month? Ideally, 20 percent of money in.

Sustain: What are your fixed monthly contracts and
commitments—must-pay bills, including minimums on
your credit card, mortgage, and student loans? Ideally,
60 percent of money in.

Spend: Nice-to-haves. Ideally, 20 percent of money in.

Bottom line: When you subtract money out (save + sustain +
spend) from money in, what's left?

If your bottom line is "something," then extra gold coins and
hearts for you. If not, your money story narrator is probably
giving you a slamming headache right now. It's okay. Tell her to
shhhhh for a moment.

Cash Flow Waterfall!

Remember, the goal here is to move your net worth positive.
To do so, you save as much money as you spend, including debt
and interest. That's how you move your net worth positive, even
when you have high-interest debt. Here's an example of how to
make that happen in real life.

Living in Jersey City, married couple Olivia and Matt earn

a combined net income of $10,000 a month. Following giving birth to twins, their credit card debt rose to $9,000 due to unexpected baby care expenses like hospital bills, cribs, and the night nurse Olivia needed as she transitioned back to work.

Their personal monthly *money clarity* spread read as follows (made simple, using round numbers so that you can read and understand it quickly):

Money in: $10,000
Save: $2,000
  • $1,000 a month toward their emergency fund
  • $1,000 toward their IRAs
Sustain: $7,000 a month
  • $2,000 toward their mortgage and co-op maintenance
  • $2,000 toward day care
  • $400 toward credit card debt
  • $600 toward cable and utilities
  • $1,000 toward baseline grocery and household expenses, which now includes diapers!
  • $1,000 toward car, insurance, and parking
Spend: $1,000 a month

Olivia's and Matt's emergency fund and credit card debts are in flux in the wake of two newborn babies.

Emergency fund balance: down to a dangerously low $3,000 from its high at $15,000

Credit card balance: now $9,000 at 16 percent interest, up from $3,000.

Olivia and Matt, each with beers in one hand and baby bottles in the other, assess their depleted savings and growing debt.

First, they pause their $1,000 a month combined IRA con-tributions, splitting it with $500 toward their credit card debt and $500 toward rebuilding their decimated emergency fund. Note that these figures are simplified for teaching purposes, and don't account for change in taxes. This means that their current $1,000 a month toward their emergency fund rises from $1,000 to $1,500 (save) and their credit card payment also increases from $400 to $900 a month (sustain). At this pace, within twelve months, they'll restore their emergency fund to $15,000 and pay off their credit card in full.

Their new monthly *money clarity* spread is as follows:

Save: $1,500
- All toward their emergency fund

Sustain: $7,500 a month
- Now includes $900 toward paying down credit card debt

Spend: $1,000 a month

You may be thinking, *Amanda, at 16 percent interest, shouldn't they drive that entire $1,000, the money that they had been saving toward their retirement, toward their $9,000 in debt?* No, and here's why. The fact that their debt rose from $2,000 to $9,000 so quickly while depleting their emergency fund from $15,000 down to $3,000 means they're likely to incur more debt. They just had twins! If they pay down debt while sacrificing their emergency fund, they'll continue to accrue more debt, leaving them ex-posed to even bigger cash emergencies in the future.

The growth of their net worth isn't diminished by pausing their IRA contributions, as any returns on investments they would make would be canceled out by the cost of interest pay-ments as a result of their debt.

Over twelve months, $9,000 credit card debt at 16 percent interest costs an additional $799 in fees.

IRA contributions of $1,000 a month over twelve months at 5 percent could earn $600. $799 is a greater cost than projected investment earnings. And without more emergency fund cash, you're at risk of more debt and more in fees.

Splitting your savings between your emergency fund and credit card debt is the only safe way to move forward until you are debt free. Otherwise, you may be building retirement assets, but you're reducing your net worth by spending more on interest.

Mind the Gap

Gaining *money clarity* means exploring all sides of your money: your numbers, your feelings, and your actions. Make peace with who you are and where you are. Life is full of surprises, stuff happens, but *even so* you can save more and spend less, no matter what your debt situation is. It's worth it.

Here are the ground rules for getting clear. It's not a competition with your perfect self, your sister, your coworkers, or anyone else. It's not about whether you have $20,000 in credit card debt or $200,000 in your 401(k). It's not about "fixing" your financial life in an exercise or two. It's about *seeing* what you have right now, learning and setting up what you need for the future, and identifying the gap between where you are now and where you want to be.

You do not have to immediately fix the gap between where you are today and where you want to be. It took me five years to climb out of my financial hole once I finally reorganized my life. Five whole years of agony and ecstasy as I cut deeply into my sustain budget by moving from a big house to a small apartment. If you stay with me, you're on your way to clarity. So it's against the rules to spend a moment feeling bad about your financial situation.

Money Clarity FAQ

You probably have a lot of questions for me right now. Here's some you may be asking, as well as answers.

"What bank accounts do I need?"

I recommend the following:

CHECKING ACCOUNT: Where you deposit your paycheck, or if you're freelance, your "draw." (See chapter nine.)

EMERGENCY FUND: There's a distinct power—yes, *power*— that saving money gives you. Once you *get that* in your bones, you'll look forward to saving more.

For your emergency fund, first save $1,000, then aim to cover one month of expenses. Experts say three to six months of cash. I live on planet Earth, so I say start by getting to one, then consider increasing it. If you're having trouble managing debt, chances are high that you'll be back in debt not too long after you've made a big payment to your credit cards. Your best insurance against additional debt is to split extra cash between savings and debt payments.

RETIREMENT FUND: If you're employed by a company, a 401(k) or the equivalent if it's available. If you're self-employed, your own IRA.

"What if my debt makes it impossible to save?"
Dig through your bag and put coins in a jar. You just saved seventy-five cents. Next week, you'll double it. Saving is a habit, not an afterthought.

"I try to save, but I keep getting wiped out. How do I keep the faith?"
This morning, I woke up to these texts from my house cleaner:

> Your 2 cats have fleas. Your house is infested with fleas
> They jump everywhere. I cannot clean your house like this
> Risk of bringing them to my other houses
> Please call pest control and I cannot come back until you do

And good morning to you (scratch). Hours later, I'm on the hook for two vet bills, two prescriptions of Revolution flea medicine, and two visits from the exterminator, totaling at least $600. Not to mention the hours of laundry, vacuuming, and vet appointment shuttling this week and next.

You know, more or less, how much your car costs each month, and then—boom!—you dent it, now owing a $500 deductible to GEICO. So do you put it on your credit card or pay out of savings? If you're already in debt, your credit card is less ideal. And for some, tapping your emergency fund for nonemergencies can feel like a step backward.

All finely tuned spending plans get blown to bits by unexpected events. To proactively manage the demoralizing events
that wipe out your savings, you can also set up a bank account
just for curveballs, aptly named a curveball fund. For every paycheck, transfer $200 into it until it reaches $500. I expect my
curveball fund to get wiped out, but by having one, which I will
use this week to pay the vet and exterminator, I'm not drawing
down another bank account, like my emergency fund or money
otherwise allocated to bills.

Keep a maximum of $500 in a curveball account, expecting
to wipe it out every three months or so. Money you put in any
savings account will make it less desirable to spend. It's a psychological trick I play on myself so that I keep my credit card
as low as possible, my confidence high, and my emergency fund
growing.

"Why so many savings accounts?"

Remember, if your day-to-day control already works for you, no
need to open a curveball fund or avoid credit cards. I know how
many women today feel bad about how hard it is to control your
cash flow. Were 1950s housewives better? Have we forgotten
some ancient wisdom known by women who preceded us? The
problem is this: because budgeting, like dieting, is restrictive,
it feeds a pass/fail mentality. Will you forgo spending $75 on a
friend's birthday dinner out this week (pass) or not (fail)? It's her
fortieth? Too bad, you have to choose: do you love your friend
or your budget more? You're left with the impression that you're
bad with money. And without the caffeine indulgence (because
you skipped the latte), you're grumpier and more uptight than

ever. Then you quit. These strategies are to help you with the big stuff as you drill down on why you're spending 40 percent of your net income on . . . well, maybe you're not sure.

"Where should I open these accounts?"
If you're happy with your bank now, as long as you're crystal clear regarding sneaky transaction fees and overdraft fees, stay. In the meantime, also consider online-only banks. The first Internet bank was established in 1995. Safe to say, they are changing our personal banking options. And, yes, they are safe to use and fully FDIC insured, just like commercial and not-for-profit banks. Some ones you may have heard of are Capital One 360, Ally, Aspiration, FNBO Direct, and even Schwab. The upsides to Internet-based banks can be pretty significant once you validate: better interest rates, more no-fee accounts, total convenience via their websites and mobile apps, robust features that actually help you with your money management (bucketing or budgeting) and financial forecasting, 24/7 customer service, free online bill paying, and even tax return preparation.

Your Turn

What's your cash flow waterfall? Where will you open accounts? In some ways, it's very simple. You'll be mesmerized by what's possible when you visualize your cash flow moving from account to account. And you could be confronted by somewhat daunting hurdles.

Karell Roxas uses the bucket system for managing her savings, and an app to track her spend budget. Both help her stay financially awake in the moment. "Sometimes before I even make a decision, I'll look at my app," she says. "If I see that I only have twenty dollars to spend for the next three days, I'm not going to take a taxi instead of the subway, or whatever I thought I might do. That was a mind-set shift for me." Karrell realized that imposing general limits on her spending gave her a lot of control and power. If her spend number was $150 a week, she really could blow $100 on a Saturday if she wanted to, then live frugally for the rest of the week. "That feels freer to me than spending recklessly and realizing too late that I am overdrawn."

Meet my friend Josh. He has made about $150,000 a year as a technology administrator (yes, that's a lot), but not because he was in a fancy job or by starting his own business. Last year at age thirty-six he surpassed $1 million in savings. How in the world did he do that? True, he belongs to a class of people known as "supersavers," but he's not superhuman. The reason he saved so much in just fifteen years of working is that he always prioritized saving and investing alongside having a consistent income. In fact, he created a game out of always choosing the least expensive option without sacrificing his happiness, like ordering the less expensive entrée on the menu, or renting the apartment twenty blocks past the "desirable" neighborhood.

Don't throw your book at me. I'm not suggesting you've done anything wrong by not being like Josh or for enjoying your life. And I'm not saying this is a gender thing. It's not. Men are no better or worse at managing money than women. It's a matter of perspective. The difference is Josh never saw his income as a sign of his personal prosperity: he simply embraced saving money alongside spending it. Spending money can be fun, and so can saving.

Let It Flow

Suppressing real emotions is not helpful.

Whenever more details come to light about the money you have coming in or going out, you can adjust these numbers. Whenever your situation changes, such as when you get a new job with a new salary, your rent or mortgage changes, you get married or divorced, or you remembered you have student loans—keep your numbers current.

Sometimes you blow your spend number—variable costs by their definition are unpredictable. If you're in cringe mode after looking at your money in and money out, get ready to scramble. Tell your money story to chill. Remember, this is not about shaming yourself, regressing or sliding into a money coma for spending. It's about getting clear. *Looking.* But if your money story is really coming on strong, you get five minutes to feel horrible. Set a timer. You can use the stopwatch function on your phone, a kitchen timer, your alarm clock—whatever is handy. You are allowed to feel like a loser for five full minutes. You can even lie on the floor and moan. How horrible you are!

But when the timer rings, you are done. Get up off the floor, unclench your fists, take a deep breath. The key to getting in the game is not giving up when you hit a roadblock. That includes emotional ones. Whatever you did in the past is done. No judgment. The future starts now. Let's get back in the game.

You will know that your financial life is working when you stay awake to the numbers, even when a giant curveball eats your emergency fund for breakfast. You're not shooting for some abstract future when you are suddenly, miraculously controlling your spending, or funding your retirement goals perfectly. You'll have periods where you are, and stretches where you aren't. The ultimate goal is to get engaged and stay engaged. Little by little, step by step, knowing that you are already managing your money, you will develop the confidence and motivation to make the bigger changes that lead you to a positive and growing net worth. For now, you're just going to look and take stock. Trust me, even taking stock can get emotional.

So let me just say this: aim right now to understand if your financial life is working. That means that you understand money in, money out, and your bottom line. Your money out consists of save, sustain, and spend. You're using these funds to grow your savings and retirement fund, and maybe buy a house or start a business. Being your own money manager means understanding that you're spending money on what truly matters to you.

Jen Turrell is a rancher in Arizona. Jen already owned property and did the taxes for the ranch business when I met her. She wasn't asleep to money. But she still worried about providing for her two autistic children, who will need ongoing care for the rest of their lives. How would she ever manage it? When she and I looked at her accounts and assets, Jen realized that she wasn't as far away from financial security as she feared. She looked at what she had square on. "It gave me a better sense of peace knowing that, even in the worst-case scenario, there would be enough to sustain my kids for a number of decades," she said to me. Looking, knowing, and understanding are very powerful things. Jen went on to establish services in her rural area for autistic kids and their parents.

Plenty of Trouble

Think of it this way: savings are deferred spending. You are eventually going to spend that money you put aside today, whether it's on a trip to see your grandma, or to fund your life when you *are* a grandma. The point is to set goals that allow you to do both. How, you may ask, is this even possible when your sustain numbers all but clean you out every month? Or maybe you think you're the worst-case spender anyone has ever seen—a hopeless case. You're not.

Here's a little background. According to the Federal Reserve Bank of St. Louis, Americans' rate of personal saving has been steadily declining since the mid-1990s. In late 2015, Americans were only saving 5.6 percent as opposed to an average of 9 percent in the early '90s and 12 percent in the early '70s. The numbers show that as a country we value saving less and less. The 2008–2009 recession inspired people to save again, but that didn't last. As our memories of the financial stock market crisis fade, we've gone back to our spending ways. And experts are not sure why.

What this means for you is that there's been less support— culturally—for the idea and practice of saving. It's fallen away. When your friends, family, and coworkers are not that concerned with saving, implementing your own plan can feel like you're swimming against the current. This can make it harder to save. But one thing finance experts come back to again and again is this: a winning formula for being financially healthy is to spend less and save more. Simple.

Being Your Own Backer

Saving money is extremely powerful. It's an opportunity you don't want to miss. If a really cool and generous person said, hey, you know that surprise medical bill from last month? Let me cover that for you. Car needs emergency repairs? Not a problem—you can put that credit card away. You want to buy a house? Have a baby? I've got this covered for you. How would that feel? All these spend events are normal. Yet often when they land in our laps, we're not ready to deal with them. But there is a way to deal with them. That way is called saving. You can be your own caped hero, swooping in for the awesome save. How cool is that? Let me answer that for you: it's very cool. Every time you don't overspend or get into debt, you can save more.

Here are two powerful reasons why you want to become a saver.

1. **Saving changes how you view money.** When your brain sees what you can afford to spend, it assumes that's all you have to work with. Even though it's *you* who set this whole system up, and *you* who controls how much is transferred from your sustain to your save accounts, you actually do start acting differently. Your priorities change. It's as if someone is helping you out. Saving automatically becomes protection from spending mindlessly since you believe you have less cash to work with. And we all need help with that.

2. **Saving gives you choices.** Saving is at the heart of the wings idea in this book. Wings help you fly, feel free, and enjoy the ride. Savings give you the power to do things that you haven't planned for, whether that's an unexpected

snowboarding trip or a kitchen renovation. Without savings
on hand, you would either forgo the fun or you would go
into debt to participate.

Women are under so much pressure internally and externally to
do it all and do it perfectly that adding a layer of austerity can
feel demoralizing. Unless you need an extreme fix, and some of
us do. In that case, austerity might be the way for you. Becoming
a saver does not mean you will never buy nice things for yourself, your home, or your kids ever again. That's a leftover idea
from the "pass/fail" diet mentality.

You're going to make more of an impact—and free up more
money to save—when you reduce the costs of big-ticket items
like rent or mortgage payments, expensive cell phone data pack-
ages, or car insurance policies than if you nickel and dime yourself without any real benefit on the other side. Unhappiness is
not motivating. It doesn't work. So allow yourself your coffee
and some new underwear. Keep your eye on your roots. That's
what will keep you motivated to save.

Design Your Life, Fund Your Dreams.

In the fall of 2015, I promised my six-year-old daughter, Maya, that she could come with me to New York, where DailyWorth's offices were located at the time. Maya knew that I often left our house in Philadelphia at dawn to head to work. At 6:03 a.m. on October 4, she was dressed, with her shoes on and her backpack full of stuffies. Most mornings I have to yell, "Wake up, child!" and flick the lights on and off. Not today. She was waiting for me by the door. We arrived in New York around noon. I had secured child care, via www.theli.st, a networking platform for women. Jessica Randazza, a major marketing executive, had volunteered to play with Maya for an hour while I had an important lunch meeting with financial journalist Jean Chatzky at 30 Rock. So far, so good. I was making Maya's dreams come true, while meeting my work responsibilities and networking with übercompetent colleagues. At least on paper. Or, rather, e-mail. Or, rather, in my mind.

In reality, getting to 30 Rock was a disaster. I was in heels, carrying my laptop, my overnight bag, and Maya's backpack. We had cabbed it most of the way, but there was a last stretch to walk before actually arriving. Maya wasn't interested in walking. Once on the sidewalk, she decided she was too tired and sat down. Weighted down with bags, both of which kept sliding off my shoulders, I couldn't pick her up. *Why* hadn't I brought flat shoes? *Why* had I thought this was a good idea? My meeting was supposed to start in minutes. Then she suddenly popped up from the sidewalk and sped away. Manically scanning the crowd, I spotted her slurping water out of the public fountain on Sixth Avenue. "Maya!" I shouted at the top of my lungs, as I lurched over to her. *"We don't lick fountains!"*

Fast-forward to the DailyWorth offices. Surprise: you can't take a kid to work and expect the team to concentrate! Maya strutted around, pressing stickers on everyone and barking, "You're fired!" So. Not. Funny. Meanwhile, my in-box was piling up. "Never again!" I groaned. And yet, yes, again. The following day, I was on a money panel for Claudia Chan's SHE Summit, a women's business and leadership conference. It was at the 92nd Street Y in uptown Manhattan. I'd asked ahead of time if I could bring Maya and leave her in the greenroom while I went onstage. The organizers thought it was a great idea. But by the time we arrived, bags and all, way uptown, Maya was beside herself. I'd dragged her around for almost two days at this point. She was *done.* In the greenroom, my fellow panelists wanted to hug and spoil her. Maya wasn't having it. She kicked a speaker in the shins and then curled into a ball in the corner. Fantastic. After my panel, Maya started screaming. *Shrieking.* I couldn't talk to anyone. We left immediately for the train. Time to go home.

Okay, in hindsight, Maya wasn't really ready for that trip— and neither was I. If I look at it in the right way, it was comical.

But I meant well. I wanted to show my daughter where Mommy goes every day. Not just the work women *do*, or to fill in the missing pieces of where Mommy goes in such a flurry, or why I sometimes work so late. I wanted Maya to see what moms at work *look like*: in charge, earning money, bringing big ideas to life. I want her to see *me* in charge, so that *she* can be in charge. I want her to see that she has the power to decide whatever she wants for herself and to have control over her own life. My daughter shouldn't have to constantly question her judgment. I want her to grow up knowing her worth, knowing how to assess what *she* wants, and knowing how to ask not *Can I? Should I?* but *Is it worth it?* and *What is it worth to me?* Very different questions, and ones we should all be asking. That's the point of this book.

What Is It Worth to *Me*?

What is worth it to *you* to be in charge of your money, your life? What are *your* terms, and are you living them? I still want to model for my daughter what a life of no regrets looks like. Sure, it can be messy and challenging. But it can also be incredibly exciting. My mom could never have taken me with her to work and integrated me into her day like that. She always had to keep me separated. That was then. Today things are far from perfect. Just a few years ago, when my son had a fever, I couldn't reschedule a big call with an influential venture capitalist. I couldn't admit to being a mom without bone-chilling fear that I'd be judged as incapable. But I've been shifting that, because being a mom is key to my life's terms—as are being a business owner, connector, and risk taker.

For you, life on your terms could mean actually admitting

that you *are* ambitious. Or it could mean taking care of yourself financially without feeling that you're selfish. Or, if you love fashion as art, it might mean buying a dress that others would see as egregious. And you're also moving money into your savings or investment accounts and building a real financial foundation at the same time. The point is this: women *can* use money to build nourishing lives that work for *us*. We *can* care about money. Wherever we go, we *can* ask, "What is it *worth* to me?" Whether it's opening long-ignored statements, or asking for a higher salary, or talking candidly with our partners about money, we can stay engaged. We know in our guts that managing money plays a crucial part in our power and security. And it's not something we want to give away.

I have learned to be in charge, and so can you. That's why I took Maya to New York. That's why I declined an invitation to the White House because I hadn't seen my kids in a few days. I want my children to see what it looks like to design my own life in service of what works for me, and us as a family, even as I work, network, and produce. I want others to see that I'm a mom and I'm not hiding it. My terms. Being in charge means that you have the power to decide whatever you want for yourself and that you have the ability to fund those desires. You're here, making changes to your life based on what *you* decide is important and what you want for your future. *You* are our world's future money leader. Yes, *you*.

We can do this now. But we still need to recognize the position of power we're already in and use our dollars to direct that. Because when we control money, we also get to rewrite rules: the way our institutions work, the way child care works, the structure of the workday, the baseline for adulthood (do you really

have to get married to be a grown-up?). We get to demand that public policies and social services actually serve us humans, not faceless mandates. We don't have to conform to outdated ideals that no longer make sense.

I hope you have seen that your personal and financial values don't have to be in conflict after all. Your money story can become positive, and so can your net worth. You can awaken from your money coma and invest in your own dreams. You don't have to wait for someone else to make money less icky. Money is yours to enjoy fully—and you can. Freedom is in your hands. That's the world I want my daughter to grow up in—and the one you can occupy right now.

Much Better Prepared

I've said this before, but it's worth saying again: by 2030, two-thirds of personal wealth in the US will be in the hands of women. Two-thirds. That's about $22 trillion. A lot. It's a dramatic shift, it's happening now, and it affects all of us. Not just our kids or grandkids—but us, *right now.* But it won't matter who holds the purse strings, or how much money we have, if we're in money comas. If we continue to think that managing money is unfeminine, continue to blindly delegate to the men or financial advisors in our lives, then the way money is spent, invested, and taxed on a national scale may not change. Because we'll still be operating from a place of avoidance. We'll still be flirting with our money comas. And this will be a huge missed opportunity.

Engaging with your money consistently and without shame is what we're after. That doesn't mean your money story won't pop up or that curveballs will stop coming your way. Or that

you won't have some significant responses to your money story or to the curveballs. Because you will. It's just that now you will be much better prepared. You'll be able to respond flexibly and creatively instead of getting freaked out. You identified your money story. Maybe that shook you up. It's a powerful first step. Now, you're going to get to see when it comes up and how persistent it is. That also means recognizing when you've slipped into a money coma. Because, believe me, you will. Things don't change overnight. It also means helping yourself to come out of your money coma with a minimum of shame and self-loathing. No matter what crap your money story throws at you, you have to know that you're not a horrible person or "bad at money" if you've checked out for a second.

Even today, I continue to remind myself that I'm a saver (my money story is I'm a spender). When I start becoming unconscious, I take action to prove to myself that I'm awake, such as moving $100 into my savings account. It helps to switch me back into responsibility mode. Small, consistent actions build integrity, I've learned. Keep practicing.

Ready for Anything

Keeping an eye on our money stories and money comas is the internal piece of the puzzle. The external piece is managing the curveballs. They're real. I'll tell you a story about a big curveball that came my way not long ago. In 2013, DailyWorth went through a devastating period of cash challenges. It put us on the brink of collapse. That was a very, very snowy winter, and a lot of investor meetings had been canceled as a result. Our ac-

counts were running dangerously low. My head of sales was out on maternity leave, and my next-in-line saleswoman—who had been doing a phenomenal job—quit with $500,000 in pending contracts to close. We weren't going to make payroll or cover our operating costs. And we had no prospects to recover the shortfall.

I was scared. I was pretty sure that our board of directors would vote to sell DailyWorth, my dream business, rather than watch it go bankrupt. But I really didn't want it to slide into foreign hands, jeopardizing its mission of making money truly engaging for women. I didn't want to lose right at the moment when we were just starting to win. Standing in my hotel room the night before the board meeting, staring at the flickering lights of the Manhattan skyline, I agonized over what to do. And then, I had an epiphany. I figured out an even better sales plan. It would start putting money in our accounts immediately, and would be a consistent model for profits going forward. I was right at that very scary razor's edge when I reinvented the revenue model for DailyWorth. My board thought I was crazy: "We appreciate your passion, Amanda, but we think you're grasping at straws." I asked them for six weeks to turn things around. And you know what? It worked. We made it.

We made it because I'm a hard charger. But we also made it because I had personal savings, could afford to go off salary, and tamed my money story so that I could reinvent our business in just a few months. Even in a terrified state, I could turn tragedy into opportunity. The board of directors reversed their decision to sell the company. What was a full-on crisis triggered the rebirth of a better business model.

A Success Story

Everyone gets into tight spots. A lot of financial advice out there says start young. It's true: we should all start young. But if you didn't, you're not a hopeless case. Remember, it wasn't too late for my mom when she got divorced at age forty-two with no skills in the 1980s. It's not too late for you now. If you wrestle yourself out of your money coma, you can do it, too. Knowing how much money and assets you have, where they are, what you can do with them, and how much more you could grow them— that's power. You're a mom, a wife, a girlfriend, a career woman, and now you *know*.

Not everyone will love your new knowledge set. Your parents, your friends, your social circle, even your kids might be puzzled by your confidence. But if you weren't happy before now—if you felt insecure—then you *have* to step up. There are millions of other women out there who are on the same journey. They will show up for you. Your world is about to get bigger and better in a radical way. When you make choices toward the life that you want to live, things get clear. People organize themselves around *you* instead of the other way around.

If I can come back from $90,000 in debt to build positive net worth, so can you. I want to be clear that life won't suddenly stop throwing you massive curveballs just because you read this book. Your money story won't just—poof!—disappear. Life— and our brains—doesn't work like that. If you are now making 401(k) contributions while also building liquid savings, brava! You have bigger wings and can fly higher than you did before. But even more important is the resilience you are going to build as you trust yourself to navigate life's ups and downs. To do that, you come to realize that managing your money is just *what you need to do.* It's like getting regular checkups and following world news. You're alive—you take care of yourself. Staying engaged with your money *is* investing in yourself. You do it because you're *worth it.*

Now is your chance to live everything you've learned. Truly, this is the fun part.

WORTH IT: Six Daily Habits

1. **Check in frequently: Is that your money story talking?** Know what drives you and what no longer serves you. Have a strategy to switch your thinking (and behavior) when your money story flares up.

2. **Prioritize saving over spending.** When you want a $400 dress, also put $400 into your savings account. That's one way to assess if you can afford the dress.

3. **Live as far below your means as possible.** Life is expensive. Cut excess and save the difference.

4. **Get clear on what's most important to you—invest in that.** Know what your dreams are. Choose roots that match your lifestyle. Spend mindfully so you can have what you really, really want in the biggest picture. Deprioritize everything else.

5. **Make sure your net worth is trending in a positive direction.** Understand how your earnings and investments affect your long-term security. Keep tweaking and growing your net worth.

6. **Remember: curveballs are the norm.** Swings in your finances don't mean you are "bad with money." They require your creativity and resilience, not your shame.

You Write the Rules

Today, we have the chance to rethink what's important to all of us. We have an opportunity to redefine how we handle money as individuals, as a country, as a culture. There's still a strong gender divide when it comes to money, but woman by woman, we can change this. What role can women play as savers, investors, and spenders in creating a world that works for everyone? To shift our economies, we first need to reconstruct our identities. We need to stop seeing ourselves as subject to larger power structures and instead see ourselves as agents of change in a global network. It's our fundamental views of who we *think* we are that prohibit us from having this conversation. Let's start it.

It's not about seeing ourselves as independent or connected. We are both—an amazing paradox. This balance of power—a deep shift in our self conception—is itself a dramatic global shift. And because women are a fresh market of investors who don't (yet) have predetermined thoughts about investing, we get to ask questions that haven't been asked in many years. What does our ideal society look like? If we could reinvent the wheel, what would it look like? What do we value? What can help to change? What do we want to influence? Do we want to fix the parental leave situation? Repair expectations for new mothers (do we need to be answering e-mails twenty minutes after giving birth)? Do we want to heal the environment? Support foreign policies that lead to poverty and displacement for millions?

Let's first get to the point where we live within our means and it's not a sacrifice. Earn more. Save deliberately. Fund ourselves and our lives. Know what we're up to financially. Then let's take down the taboo around talking about money. Let's stop feeling ashamed and avoiding the subject and actually talk frankly with our friends and our families. Let's share financial information as easily as we share tips on restaurants and child rearing. Once we start looking and taking action on our own behalf, it will be really fun to talk about it.

Collectively, women now have an unprecedented level of influence and power, more than any other time in history. Join me in using it to create a better future for our families, ourselves, and our world, together.

Summary

Formulas and Checklists

Below is a summary of what we just discussed and all the key points you need to remember. Consider this your Worth It cheat sheet!

Key Concepts
- Focus on positive net worth, not just increasing your income.
- Save to spend—before you make a major purchase, consider how much you have in savings.
- Live below your means—as far as you can.

Know Your Net Worth
- Calculate net worth by adding up your assets (cash, savings, property value, car, retirement and investment accounts) and subtracting your debts (credit cards, student loans, mortgage).

Manage Your Money

- Know your net monthly income: what do you really take home after taxes, benefits, withholdings, and other fees? If you're a freelancer, pay yourself a fixed draw, and a bonus annually.
- Stock your emergency fund: have one to three months' worth of expenses saved.
- Expect that curveballs will be the norm.

Use the Bucket System

- Use buckets and budgets. Sustain: 60 percent. Save: 20 percent. Spend: 20 percent.

Here are sample breakdowns by annual income, in round numbers.

	Annual Income	Monthly Net Income	60 % Sustain	20 % Save	20 % Spend
Minimum	$25,000	$1,500	$900	$250	$250
Basic	$50,000	$3,000	$1,800	$600	$600
Executive	$100,000	$6,000	$4,000	$1,000	$1,000
Affluent	$200,000	$10,000	$6,000	$2,000	$2,000

Home Ownership

- Spend three years or less of your annual household income on the total cost of your home.
- Factor in the total cost of home ownership:
  - Down payment
  - Closing costs
  - Initial move-in and repairs
  - Monthly utilities

- ○ Mortgage payments and interest
- ○ Property tax payments
- ○ Ongoing maintenance and renovations

Retirement & Investing
- Know your retirement goal: what's your dream number?
- Is your portfolio growing on average at least 5 percent per year? If not, investigate why.
- Asset allocation: make sure you have a diversified mix of stocks, bonds, and other asset classes.

Running a Business
- Are you building your business to have an income stream or an asset? Understand the trade-offs.
- Can you tolerate an uncertain income in exchange for no ceiling on your potential earning?
- Do you enjoy managing every aspect of your work, from solving tech issues to setting your schedule (the *free* in *freelance* is usually misleading, BTW), to finding customers and advertising your brilliance?

Congratulations, you're now equipped to design your life, on your terms, and fund it. You are WORTH IT!

Notes

1. Boston Consulting Group, 2009
2. BMO Wealth Institute, 2015
3. Boston Consulting Group: Global Wealth 2016 Report
4. "Data & Statistics: Women in the Labor Force," United States Department of Labor website, https://www.dol.gov /wb/stats/stats_data.htm
5. "Knowledge Center: Women's Earnings and Income," Catalyst website, April 8, 2016, http://www.catalyst.org /knowledge/womens-earnings-and-income#UnitedStates
6. "Women and Retirement Savings," United States Department of Labor website, https://www.dol.gov /ebsa/publications/women.html
7. "Detailed Tables on Wealth and Asset Ownership," United States Census Bureau website, http://www.census.gov /people/wealth/data/dtables.html
8. http://bmogamviewpoints.com/wp-content/uploads/2015 /04/wealth-institute-financial-concerns-of-women1.pdf
9. Shelley Correll and Caroline Simard, "Research: Vague Feedback is Holding Women Back," *Harvard Business*

Review, April 29, 2016, https://hbr.org/2016/04/research
-vague-feedback-is-holding-women-back

10. Cathleen Clerkin, Christine A. Crumbacher, Julia
Fernando, and William A. (Bill) Gentry, "Bossy: What's
Gender Got to Do With It?" Center for Creative Leadership, 2015, http://insights.ccl.org/wp-content/uploads
/2015/04/Bossy2.pdf

11. Hannah Riley Bowles, Linda Babcock, and Lei Lai, "Social
Incentives for Gender Differences in the Propensity to
Initiate Negotiations: Sometimes It Does Hurt to Ask,"
ScienceDirect, June 24, 2005, https://www.cfa.harvard.edu
/cfawis/bowles.pdf

12. "Financial Experience & Behaviors Among Women," 2014–
2015 Prudential Research Study, http://www.prudential
.com/media/managed/wm/media/Pru_Women_Study_
2014.pdf?src=Newsroom&pg=WomenStudy2014

13. Carol Dweck, "The Antidote to Our Anxious Times is a
Learning Mindset," *Harvard Business Review*, July 28, 2016,
https://hbr.org/2016/07/the-antidote-to-our-anxious-times
-is-a-learning-mindset

14. Herminia Ibarra, Robin J. Ely, Deborah M. Kolb, "Women
Rising: The Unseen Barriers," *Harvard Business Review*,
September 2013, https://hbr.org/2013/09/women-rising
-the-unseen-barriers

15. "Fifteen Facts About Women's Retirement Outlook,"
Transamerica Center for Retirement Studies, March 2015,
http://www.transamericacenter.org/docs/default-source
/resources /women-and-retirement/tcrs2015_sr_womens_
retirement_outlook.pdf

16. Elyssa Kirkham, "1 in 3 Americans Has Saved $0 for Re-

tirement," March 14, 2016, GOBankingRates, https://www
.gobankingrates.com/retirement/1-3-americans-0-saved
-retirement/

17. Guy Berger, "Will This Year's College Grads Job-Hop
More Than Previous Grads?" LinkedIn Official Blog, April
12, 2016, https://blog.linkedin.com/2016/04/12/will-this
-year_s-college-grads-job-hop-more-than-previous-grads

18. Natalie Sabadish and Monique Morrissey, "Retirement
Inequality Chartbook: How the 404(k) Revolution Created
a Few Big Winners and Many Losers," Economic Policy Institute, September 6, 2013, http://www.epi.org/publication
/retirement-inequality-chartbook/

19. "Freelancers Union and Upwork Release New Study Re-
vealing Insights Into the Almost 54 Million People Freelancing in America," Upwork, 2015, https://www.upwork
.com/press/2015/10/01/freelancers-union-and-upwork
-release-new-study-revealing-insights-into-the-almost-54
-million-people-freelancing-in-america/

20. "Women and Retirement Savings," United States Department of Labor website, https://www.dol.gov/ebsa/pdf
/women.pdf

21. Elyssa Kirkham, "1 in 3 Americans Has Saved $0 for
Retirement," March 14, 2016, GOBankingRates, https://
www.gobankingrates.com/retirement/1-3-americans-0
-saved-retirement/

22. Olga Dow, "5 Ways Part-Time Employees Can Take
Advantage of 401(k) Plans," Transamerica Center for
Retirment Studies, December 15, 2014, http://blog.trans
america.com/5-ways-part-time-employees-can-take
-advantage-401k-plans#.V1nmnpMrLdQ

23. Joe Coughlin, "Do Men and Women View Retirement Differently?" Ameriprise Financial https://www.ameriprise.com/retirement/insights/joe-coughlin/how-men-women-view-retirement/

24. Elyssa Kirkham, "1 in 3 Americans Has Saved $0 for Retirement," March 14, 2016, GOBankingRates, https://www.gobankingrates.com/retirement/1-3-americans-0-saved-retirement/

25. Theresa Ghilarducci and Hamilton E. James, "A Smarter Plan to Make Retirement Savings Last," *New York Times*, January 1, 2016, http://www.nytimes.com/2016/01/02/opinion/a-smarterplan-to-make-retirement-savings-last.html?rref=collection%2Ftimestopic%2FSocial Security (US)&action=click&contentCollection=timestopics&region=stream&module=stream_unit&version=latest&contentPlacement=9&pgtype=collection&_r=1

26. Anna Bernasek, "The Typical Household, Now Worth a Third Less," *New York Times*, July 26, 2014, http://www.nytimes.com/2014/07/27/business/the-typical-household-now-worth-a-third-less.html

27. "Insight 5: 'Bag Lady' Fears Persist Even Among the Most Successful Women," Allianz website, 2016, https://www.allianzlife.com/retirement-and-planning-tools/women-money-and-power/bag-lady

28. Fidelity Viewpoints, "Women & Money: How to Take Charge," Fidelity website, March 23, 2016, https://www.fidelity.com/viewpoints/personal-finance/women-manage-money

29. Julia Sonenshein, "Women Actually Aren't Afraid of Invest-

ing, DailyWorth, March 17, 2016, https://www.dailyworth
.com/posts/4222-women-feel-left-out-of-investing

30. Mark Chussil, "Slow Deciders Make Better Strategists," *Harvard Business Review*, July 8, 2016, https://hbr
.org/2016/07/slow-deciders-make-better-strategists

31. "The Issue of Leaving a Legacy," HSBC website, April
29, 2015, http://www.hsbc.com/news-and-insight/insight
-archive/2015/the-issue-of-leaving-a-legacy

32. "Financial Experience & Behaviors Among Women," 2014
–2015 Prudential Research Study, https://www.cgsnet.org
/ckfinder/userfiles/files/Pru_Women_Study.pdf

33. Libby Kane, "Why Women Can Make the Best
Investors," LearnVest, March 23, 2012, https://www
.learnvest.com/knowledge-center/why-women-can-make
-the-best-investors/

34. Adi Ignatius, "Making Startups More Resilient," *Harvard
Business Review*, March 2016, https://hbr.org/archive-toc
/BR1603

35. Robert Wood and Albert Bandura, "Impact of Conceptions
of Ability on Self-Regulatory Mechanisms and Complex
Decision Making," *Journal of Personality and Social Psychology*, Vol. 56, No. 3.407–415, 1989, http://web.stanford.edu
/dept/psychology/bandura/pajares/Bandura1989JPSP.pdf

Index